Fountain Series in Law and Business Studies

Offences Against the Person
Homicides and
Non-fatal Assaults
in Uganda

Lillian Tibatemwa-Ekirikubinza

Fountain Publishers

Fountain Publishers Ltd
P.O. Box 488
Kampala, Uganda
Email: fountain@starcom.co.ug
Website: www.fountainpublishers.co.ug

Distributed in Europe, North America and Australia by African Books Collective (ABC), The Jam Factory, 27 Park End St, Oxford OX1 1HU, United Kingdom. Tel: 44(0) 1865-726686, Fax:1865-793298

© Lillian Tibatemwa-Ekirikubinza 2005
First published 2005

ISBN   9970 02 477 9

Acknowlegements

I am grateful to the Faculty of Law, Makerere University for the funds which enabled me to carry out the research for this book.

Cataloguing-in-Publishing Data

Tibatemwa Ekirikubinza, Lillian
Offences against the person: homicides and non fatal assaults.– Kampala: Fountain Publishers, 2005
__ p. __ cm

ISBN 9970 02 477 9

1. Criminal Law – Uganda   2. Homicides – Uganda
I. Lillian Tibatemwa- Ekirikubinza.   II. Title

364

Dedication

To my friend and husband Paul – thank you for always bringing out the best in me. And to my sons, Emmy, Joshua and Elisha – I am challenged by your consistent question: 'Mum, when are you writing another book?'

Contents

List of Abbreviations

Law Reports
AC: Appeals Cases
All ER: All England Reports
CLR: Commonwealth Law Reports
Cox CC: Cox's Criminal Law Cases
Crim App Rep: Criminal Appeal Reports
Crim LR: Criminal Law Revision
EA: East African Law Reports
EACA: East African Court of Appeal Cases
EALR: East African Law Reports
ER: England Reports
HCB: High Court Bulletin
HCCSC: High Court Criminal Session
KB: King's Bench
QB: Queen's Bench
QBD: Queens Bench Division
ULR: Uganda Law Reports
WLR: Weekly Law Reports

Preface

This is a textbook on the *substantive* law of homicide and non-fatal assaults in Uganda. It is based on judicial interpretation of the Uganda Penal Code – the principal criminal legislation of the country.[1] Although the major purpose of the book is a discussion of the major offences created by the Penal Code Act, I have included expositions on some rules of evidence in so far as it is necessary for an understanding of substantive criminal law.

In 1930 Britain introduced a Model Criminal Code in several of its colonies, Uganda inclusive. Although the Uganda Penal Code in its present form is still principally a reflection of criminal law as it existed in Britain in 1930, over the years the Uganda Judiciary has interpreted principles of criminal law based on our society's political, cultural, social and economic circumstances, and thereby developed its own jurisprudence. In some cases this has led to fundamental departures from English judge-made law. It is thus necessary to record the law as it is interpreted and understood within the Ugandan context. Consequently, the book is a result of a perusal of records of the High Court of Uganda, the Court of Appeal and the Uganda Supreme Court. Focus was limited to decisions at these three levels of the judiciary because it is these courts which are courts of record. This means that their decisions are binding on lower courts.

It is however noted that up to the early 1970s, Uganda, Kenya and Tanzania shared the services of a joint appellate court: the Court of Appeal for Eastern Africa. Although the court was only an appellate court from where decisions of the national High Courts of each country were reconsidered, its decisions as the highest court in all the three countries were binding in all the three jurisdictions. The reader will thus notice extensive use in the book of judgements by the East African Court of Appeal.

At the time of independence for Uganda, Kenya, Tanganyika, Malawi and Zambia the criminal codes of these countries were almost identical. They were all a result of the Model Criminal Code introduced into each of these countries in 1930 by the British colonial 'masters'. Each country has over the years made changes to their law. Some changes have been in the form of the creation of new offences[2], others have constituted amendments to already existing offences.[3] Nevertheless one can confidently say that the penal codes are still in *pari materia*. It is, however, unfortunate that in each of these countries there is hardly any book on substantive criminal law based on the statutory provisions as interpreted by the national courts of the independent states.

Teachers of criminal law in each of these countries still refer students to criminal law books based on English law such as Card, Cross and Jones; Smith and Hogan. Books coming out of England today are based on the current English law. Yet England has

---

[1] Chapter 120 of the Laws of Uganda, Revised Edition, 2000. Originally Chapter 106.
[2] In Uganda examples include Statute 4 of 1990 which created new sexual offences and also altered the ingredients of some existing offences. The Statute also created the offence of issuing a bounced cheque. The offence of terrorism was created in 2002.
[3] In Uganda for example the law relating to defilement of an underage girl has been substantially changed as is discussed in the volume on Sexual Assaults and Offences against Morality.

consistently come up with new statutes on different aspects of criminal law and consequently the current English law is often very different from the 'English' law introduced into colonial Africa in 1930. And as already mentioned the independent states too come up with new statutes which represent a departure from English law, not just as introduced in 1930 but also different from the current English law. These developments (in England and in the independent states) make books coming out of England today, more and more irrelevant to the jurisprudence of South-Eastern Africa. This book is designed to fill that gap. It will offer invaluable reading not only to students and scholars of the law on crime in Uganda but also to students in the other sister countries.

In presenting what the law is, I am keenly aware that whereas it may be obvious that offences such as murder, theft and assaults are injurious to individuals as well as to society as a whole, and are thus deserving of being criminalised, there may be disagreements on whether 'victimless' crimes such as incest between adults, prostitution, homosexuality, sedition, attempted suicide, etc. should be punished by the criminal law. Where possible I have (albeit briefly) presented the views of groups which support criminalisation, and also those which support decriminalisation of the relevant conduct.

I further note that there is need to analyse criminal law in the light of the wider policy issues of contemporary society. This will help students and scholars appreciate the law within Uganda's specific context. In discussing some of the offences therefore I have, *inter alia* made reference to the significance of issues such as:
- Gender and Women's Human Rights
- Children's Rights
- Human Rights
- Constitutionalism

The book is therefore not just a presentation of substantive law, but in addition it answers questions of how wider policy issues have impacted or should impact on criminal law. Hopefully, students will come out better prepared to deal with issues of law reform, especially from a human rights perspective.

The reader will note that in the presentation of each case I indicate the level of court at which the particular decision was made. This is of value in light of the principle of judicial precedent. Each court is bound by the decisions of the court above it. Thus the decision of the High Court binds all magistrates' courts. A decision of the Court of Appeal binds itself and all lower courts i.e. High Court and Magistrates' Courts. By tradition individual judges of the High Court are not absolutely bound by the decisions of other high court judges, but in practice they usually follow such decisions. This is because judicial courtesy requires that a judge does not *lightly* dissent from the considered opinion of another learned judge. Decisions of the Supreme Court bind itself and all the lower courts, i.e. the Court of Appeal, the High Court and all Magistrates' Courts. As long as no higher court has departed from the interpretation of the law by a lower court, the interpretation of that lower court remains the law. This arises out of the doctrine of *stare decisis* which means that the courts abide by former precedents where the same points of law arise again in litigation.

The system of judicial precedent is dependent upon the existence of good law reporting. Each year the courts of record hear thousands of cases, but the state of law reporting in Uganda is unsatisfactory. Consequently, although the main targets of the publication are students and scholars of criminal law, there is no doubt that the book will be invaluable to judicial officers and practising lawyers.

I must also make mention of the fact that direct quotations of sections of the Penal Code Act by the author are according to Chapter 120 Laws of Uganda, Revised Edition 2000. However, references to sections of the law in court judgements are references to sections as they stood before publication of the revised laws.

Lillian Tibatemwa-Ekirikubinza
December 2004

1
Introduction

This book deals with the substantive law on offences involving physical violence[1] against the individual. It deals with assaults which culminate in death as well as with non-fatal assaults – assaults which do not end in death.

I discuss seven different types of homicides and, with the use of case law, bring out the characteristics of each type. The different categories of homicides discussed are:

1. Murder under Sections 188, 189 and 191 Uganda Penal Code
2. Manslaughter under Sections 187 and 190 Uganda Penal Code
3. Manslaughter under Sections 192 and 193 Uganda Penal Code
4. Suicide Pacts under Section 195 Uganda Penal Code
5. Diminished Responsibility under Section 194 Uganda Penal Code
6. Infanticide under Section 213 Uganda Penal Code

The offences closely related to homicides are:

1. Attempt to Murder under Section 204 Uganda Penal Code.
2. Procuring a Miscarriage (Abortion) under Sections 141-143 Uganda Penal Code
3. Killing an unborn Child under Section 212 Uganda Penal Code

The non-fatal assaults discussed are:

1. Common Assault under Section 235 Uganda Penal Code
2. Assault causing Actual Bodily Harm under Section 236 Uganda Penal Code.
3. Doing Grievous Harm under Section 219 Uganda Penal Code.

Definition of homicide

A homicide refers to the killing of a human being by another human being. It is the act of a human being, taking away the life of another human being. A homicide is not necessarily a crime. The term merely describes the act and does not indicate the moral or legal quality of the conduct. A homicide may be lawful (and therefore not punishable) or unlawful and therefore attract penal provisions.

Lawful homicides

Examples of lawful homicides are:

Execution of a lawful sentence

Where the state executes a person who has been convicted of a criminal offence and a sentence of death has been passed by a court of competent jurisdiction under the laws of Uganda.[2] Execution is thus a homicide but one carried out as a lawful judicial sentence.

Killing in self-defence

Where a person kills another in self-defence the homicide may be ruled lawful.[3] Thus

1

in *Uganda v Sebastiano Otti* [1994-95] HCB 21, Justice Okello held *inter alia* that:

> Death is excusable when caused in self defence. To constitute self defence there must have been an unlawful attack on the accused who as a result reasonably believed that he was in eminent danger of death or serious bodily harm and it was necessary for him to use force to repel the attack made upon him. Also the force used by the accused must have been reasonably necessary to prevent the threatened danger.

Conclusion: A successful plea of self defence therefore leads to an acquittal.
See also *Uganda V Dick Ojok* [1992-93] HCB 54

Killing in defence of property
CASE: In *Marwa s/o Robi* v R [1959] EA 660
The appellant was convicted of murder for spearing to death the deceased after a dispute over cattle which the deceased claimed and had gone to the appellant to collect. On appeal it was assumed in the appellant's favour that the deceased had gone to reclaim cattle to which he had no legitimate claim and that the deceased actually attempted to drive away the cattle. The trial judge had found that no force was used against the appellant, although the deceased had carried a stick when he went towards the appellant's boma. On appeal it was *inter alia* argued for the appellant that the trial judge misdirected himself as to the law applicable to cases of homicide in defence of property.

Issue: Whether killing in defence of property justified under Section 18 of the Kenya Penal Code Act (Equivalent of Section 15 of The Uganda Penal Code Act).

Held *inter alia*: It must be a question of fact in each case whether the degree of force used in defence of property which caused death was, in the particular circumstances of the case, justifiable.

Conclusion: From this case one can conclude that where the force used is justifiable, a person who kills another in defence of property can be acquitted of a charge of murder.

CASE: In *Uganda v Fabiano* Criminal Session Case No. 161/1972 (High Court):
The accused was acquitted of murder on a successful plea of self defence.
On the material evening, the accused was informed by a neighbour that someone had entered his house. The accused rushed home and on arrival in his house, the deceased ran and collided with him in the dark, both of them falling down. The accused got up, picked a hatchet from nearby and hit the deceased on the head and leg. The deceased died instantly of a crushed skull. The accused pleaded that he was acting in self defence and in defence of his property from the hand of an unknown thief.

Held *inter alia*:
• That the accused, like any other person, was expected to guard his property against thieves using no more force than was necessary in the circumstances.
• The accused was entitled to defend his own life against the deceased by administering the blows as he thought his life was in danger. In such a

heated moment as that, it was difficult to judge what force was necessary to overcome the attacker.

Conclusion: Accused found not guilty of murder and acquitted.

Killing to prevent the commission of serious crime

Where a person kills to prevent the commission of a serious crime, such homicide may be lawful. Like the question of a killing in order to defend oneself or one's property, whether or not the killing is lawful and thus the killer is acquitted depends on the reasonableness of the force used. Under Section 2 of the Criminal Procedure Code Act, a police officer and/or any other person may use all means necessary to effect arrest. The means used may be forceful in nature. However, if the force used exceeds that which is necessary for the apprehension of the offender, the person effecting the arrest would be guilty of a crime.[4] The same rule is provided under Section 225 of the Penal Code Act.[5]

CASE: In *M'ibui v Dyer* [1967] EA 315 it was held *inter alia* by the High Court of Kenya that there is no distinction between the power of a police officer and of a private person to arrest without warrant on suspicion of a felony; and so long as there are reasonable grounds for suspicion, a private person is entitled to arrest and in doing so to use such force as is reasonable in the circumstances or is necessary for the apprehension of the offender.

Accidental killing

A successful plea of accident leads to an acquittal. Thus, the person whose conduct leads to the death is not punished. Although the killing would not be justifiable, it is excusable.

CASE: In *Obadia Kuku v Uganda*, Criminal Appeal No.5/1998. (Court of Appeal for Uganda) it was held that where an accused successfully pleads accidental killing, the verdict will be an acquittal. And that in such cases, the issue of whether excessive force was used does not arise. Such only arises if the accused pleads self defence.

CASE: *Quininto Etum v Uganda*, Criminal Appeal 19/1989. (Supreme Court).
The Supreme Court cited Gusambiza Wesonga (1948) 15 E.A.C.A 65 where it was stated that homicide accidentally caused is not unlawful, a person cannot be criminally held responsible for an act carried out accidentally.

CASE: *Uganda v Lazaro Daniel Idubale* Criminal Session Case No.84/95 (High Court)
The law makes accident an absolute defence. Section 8 (1) of the Uganda Penal code absolves a person from criminal responsibility for an act or omission which occurs independently of the exercise of his will or an event which occurs by accident.

And where an accused sets up any defence, the duty is upon the prosecution to negative the defence. Thus in *Uganda v Sempija Samuel* Criminal Case No. 243/98, the High Court stated that the onus of proving that the event was intended and not by accident lies on the prosecution.

Unlawful homicides

All homicides are presumed unlawful although the presumption is rebuttable. As put by Justice Okello in *Uganda v Bosco Okello alias Anyanya* [1992-93] HCB 68:

> There is a presumption that a homicide is unlawful unless excused by law, but the presumption can be rebutted by evidence of accident or that it was permitted in the circumstances.

The learned judge went further to say that the burden to rebut the presumption is on the accused and the standard is on a balance of probabilities.

The same principle was laid out in *Uganda v Geoffrey Saaku* Criminal Case No. 112/97. Citing *R v Busembezi Wesonga* (1948) 15 EACA 65, Justice Mukanza held *inter alia* that a homicide unless accidental is always unlawful except when committed in circumstances making it excusable.

See also *Uganda v Dick Ojok* [1992-3] HCB 54 where it was held that it is now an accepted principle of law that death of a human being unless accidental or caused in circumstances which are excusable by law is presumed to be unlawful.

Even where a homicide is unlawful, the law's reaction to a specific homicide depends on the circumstances surrounding the homicide/killing. Homicidal offences are distinguished either by the state of mind (*mens rea*) accompanying the act of killing, or in others, by the availability of mitigating factors which the law makes available to a person who would otherwise be guilty of murder. Some homicides are punished more harshly than others.

---

1. I am aware that offences which involve sexual assaults are inherently a violation of the victim's bodily integrity and are often violent in nature. Nevertheless, sexual offences are imbued with dynamics that differ from other violent assaults. Consequently I have dealt with sexual offences in a separate book.
2. Article 22 (1) of Uganda's 1995 Constitution provides: No person shall be deprived of life intentionally except in execution of a sentence passed in a fair trial by a court of competent jurisdiction in respect of a criminal offence under the laws of Uganda and the conviction and sentence have been confirmed by the highest appellate court.
3. A more detailed exposition on the law of self defence is found in the section on defences to murder.
4. Section 2: (1) In making an arrest the police officer making the same shall actually touch or confine the body of the person to be arrested, unless there be submission to the custody by word or action. (2) If such person forcibly resists the endeavour to arrest him, or attempts to evade arrest, such police officer or other person may use all means necessary to effect the arrest: Provided that nothing in this section contained shall be deemed to justify the use of greater force than was reasonable in the particular circumstances in which it was employed or was necessary for the apprehension of the offender.
5. Any person authorised by law or by the consent of the person injured by him to use force is criminally responsible for any excess, according to the nature and quality of the act which constitutes the excess.

2
Ingredients common to all Homicides

Before a homicidal offence can be established, the following ingredients must be proved beyond reasonable doubt:
1. That the victim (deceased) was a human being
2. That death *in fact* occurred
3. That the victim died within a year and a day of the unlawful act/omission causing the death
4. That the conduct (act or omission) complained of must have been unlawful
5. That it was the conduct of the accused that caused/led to the victim's death

The victim must be a human being

Who is a human being for purposes of homicide? The question is answered by resolving two issues:
1. When does life begin for purposes of homicide/at what stage in human development is the 'foetus' capable of being 'killed'?
2. At what point of time does life end, so that the intended victim is too dead to be 'killed'?

In regard to both issues, the law is guided more by medical opinion and less by moral principles.

The beginning of life

The law of homicide protects any reasonable creature *in rerum natura* i.e. any human being. Section 197 of the Uganda Penal Code deals with the question of when a child is deemed a person, capable of being killed. According to the Section:

> A child becomes a person capable of being killed when it has completely proceeded in a living state from the body of its mother, whether it has breathed or not, and whether it has an independent circulation or not, and whether the navel string is severed or not.

Consequently, it is not homicide to destroy a baby who is not yet born alive.[1] According to Section 197, it is not necessary that the umbilical cord should have been severed. Even where this has not yet occurred, the baby would still be capable of being a victim of homicide, if she has proceeded in a living state from the body of its mother.[2]

What constitutes a living state?

This refers to the fact that the child has an existence independent of its mother. According to Smith and Hogan (1992:328) the tests of independent existence which the courts have accepted are that the child should have an independent circulation, and that it should have breathed after birth.

Breathing: The breathing test is questionable since it is a fact that some children are born alive but do not breathe for some time after their birth. It is for this reason that in the old case of *Brain*, Justice Park said: '... it is not essential that it should have breathed at the time it was killed; as many children are born alive and yet do not breathe for some time after their birth.' (1834) 6 C & P at 350. It therefore is understandable that Section 197 specifically states that a child need not have breathed after birth, for it to be deemed capable of being killed.

Independent circulation: According to Card, Cross and Jones (1992:191), there is no modern authority on what is required for an independent existence. The authors however report that earlier case law reveals that while some judges favoured the test of independent breathing, others favoured that of independent circulation, in addition to breathing. Smith and Hogan (1992: 328-9) also report that there is some uncertainty about the precise moment at which the child comes under the protection of the law. It is to be noted however that Section197 Uganda Penal Code saves judges dealing with the issue in Uganda since it specifically provides that it is not necessary to prove that the child had an independent circulation.

Injuries which occur before birth, leading to death after birth
In *Senior's* case,[3] the accused was a midwife who attended the birth of a child. During the birth the child's head became visible. The accused compressed and crushed the skull of the child before it was fully expelled from the body of the mother. The child died immediately after it was born as a result of the pre-natal injury. The court held that the conduct of the accused was sufficient for the conviction of manslaughter on the basis of gross negligence.

CASE: *A-G Reference* (No 3 of 1994)[4]
The accused stabbed his pregnant girlfriend in the back and abdomen with a long bladed knife whilst she was between 22 and 24 weeks pregnant. The girlfriend went into premature labour. The baby was born alive and lived 121 days. It was discovered that the knife had penetrated the baby's lower abdomen. The baby died after she had succumbed to broncho-pulmonary dysplasia from the effects of premature birth.
    Lord Hope stated:

> There was a respectable body of medical evidence that the child was born prematurely as a result of the stabbing, and that it was as a result of the prematurity at her birth that she died. It was not disputed that the injury to a foetus before birth which results in harm to the child when it is born can give rise to criminal responsibility for that injury. So the fact that the child was not yet born when the stabbing took place does not prevent the requirements for the *actus reus* from being satisfied in this case, both for murder and manslaughter, in regard to her subsequent death.

The end of life: has death occurred?
At what stage is a human being so 'dead' that he or she is incapable of being murdered? At what stage in the process of death does a person become a corpse? Scholars of crime seem to agree that the test is one of brain death and that this can be medically diagnosed with certainty.[5] It is to be noted that the Uganda Penal Code does not offer any legal definition of death.

Discussion point: When people are on life support machines are they really corpses or should they be treated as persons for purposes of homicide?[6]

The medical profession has accepted brain stem death as the test for determining when a patient is dead. What do the courts say?

Although Ugandan courts have not pronounced themselves on this issue, English courts have done so.

CASE: In *R v Malcherek and Steel,* [1981] 2 All ER 422 'the victim' was on a life support machine. The machine was switched off by the doctors. The court said that according to medical evidence there is only one test of death and that is the irreversible death of the brain stem which controls the basic functions of the body such as breathing. In the case of brain stem death, the body has died, even though, by medical means the lungs are caused to operate and some blood is in circulation.

CASE: In *Airedale NHS Trust v Bland*, [1993] A.C 789 (House of Lords) 'the victim' was injured as a result of the Hillsborough Football Stadium disaster. His lungs were crushed and the supply of oxygen to the brain was interrupted. He was left in a permanent vegetative state and on life support for three years. There was an application to the court by way of declarations to lawfully discontinue life-sustaining treatment and medical support designed to keep the victim alive, and to lawfully discontinue medical treatment. The court held that the sanctity of life is not violated by ceasing to give medical treatment and care involving invasive manipulation of the body, to which he had not consented and which conferred no direct benefit upon him. It was noted that further treatment was futile and that prolonging the patient's life by medical treatment could not be said to be in his best interests. The omission to perform the duty to save a life was no longer unlawful given the circumstances.

Proof of death

Before an accused can be convicted of any type of homicide, the fact of death must be proved beyond reasonable doubt. The fact of death may be proved through the following ways:
1. Production of a death certificate
2. Circumstantial evidence
3. Evidence of witnesses who saw the corpse of the deceased
4. Admission by the accused that he/she killed the victim

Proof of fact of death through production of a death certificate
Although a death certificate is accepted as proof of death, it is not always necessary for this to be reinforced by a post mortem report.

Proof of fact of death through circumstantial evidence
CASE: *Regina v Onufrejczyk* [1955] QBD 388
The appellant was convicted of the murder of his partner, who had disappeared. There was no trace of the victim's body, or direct evidence of his death, or of the way in which he died, and no confession or admission of the death by the appellant, but very strong evidence, in particular the conduct of the appellant, which showed that he knew that the victim could never appear again and that he had tried to fabricate evidence

that he was alive. On the basis of the conduct of the appellant and the fact that the victim had not been seen alive, the appellant was convicted of murder.

He appealed against the conviction. It was submitted by the appellant that unless the body can be found or an account given of the death, the law is that there is no proof of a *corpus delicti.*

Held: Chief Justice Lord Goddard and Justices Cassels and Sellers held:

> It is clear that the fact of death, like any other fact, can be proved by circumstantial evidence, that is to say, evidence of facts which lead to one conclusion, and one conclusion only, that the victim is dead. The circumstances must be so cogent and compelling as to point to no rational hypothesis other than death. ... it is indeed a grave step to find a murder proved when there is no body ... but of course, the burden of proving everything against the [accused] is on the crown.

Conclusion: In a trial for murder the fact of death can be proved by circumstantial evidence provided that the jury are warned that the evidence must lead to one conclusion only, and, therefore, notwithstanding that there is no body, or trace of a body, or any direct evidence as to the manner of death of a victim, the *corpus delicti* may be proved by such circumstances as render the commission of the crime certain and leave the jury with no degree of doubt.

CASE: *Kimweri v Republic* [1968] E.A. 452

The appellant was charged with and convicted of the murder of his wife from whom he had been separated and against whom his petition for divorce had failed. The appellant had been ordered to pay maintenance to his wife and in the meantime he had a liaison with another woman. The appellant's wife disappeared from her room on a day on which the prosecution alleged that the appellant (who had a motive to dispose of her) had visited her in Moshi and a few days later, the wife's father received a letter purporting to come from one Kamau and stating that the appellant's wife had gone to Nairobi with Kamau and that in the course of the journey she had been killed in a motor accident. Evidence was given to the effect that inquiries were made in Kenya and that these inquiries resulted in information being supplied to the witness that no such motor accident had occurred. The prosecution also sought to show that the letter was typed on a typewriter to which the appellant had access.

Held:

1. Although death may be proved by circumstantial evidence, that evidence must be such as to compel the inference of death, and must be such as to be inconsistent with any theory of the alleged deceased being alive, with the result that taken as a whole the evidence leaves no doubt whatsoever that the person in question is dead;
2. The circumstances in the present case raised a considerable suspicion that the wife was dead, but did not compel irresistibly the inference of death; the conviction was quashed and sentence set aside.

Judgement delivered by Sir Charles Newbold:

While death may be proved by circumstantial evidence, without evidence as to the production of the body of the allegedly dead person and without any evidence of a person who saw the body of the dead person and without a confession by a person accused that he caused the death, yet where a court is asked to find in a murder charge that a person is dead in the circumstances which we have stated, the evidence on which the court is asked to infer death must be such as to compel the inference of death and must be such as to be inconsistent with any reasonable theory of the alleged deceased being alive, with the result that taken as a whole, the evidence leaves no doubt whatsoever that the person in question is dead. We would give as an example of what we mean the case of a person on a ship in the middle of the ocean. Evidence is given that a scream was heard, and a splash was heard, but there is no evidence that any particular person was seen to go overboard.

This ship is searched and subsequently a person in relation to whom evidence is given that that person was a passenger on that ship is found to be missing. In those circumstances, although there was no evidence of a body, although no-one came forward and said that the body of the alleged deceased was seen and although there was no confession by anyone, nevertheless, those circumstances are such as to compel the inference of death.

The circumstances of the present case raise a considerable suspicion that the wife is dead. But we feel unable to come to the conclusion, in a criminal charge of murder, that these circumstances, suspicious as they may be, compel irresistibly the inference of death.

We are unable to say that we are satisfied beyond any possibility of doubt that the wife is dead, even though we may have the strongest suspicions to that effect.

CASE: *Uganda v Albino Ajok* Criminal. Session Case No.117 of 1974, before Justice Manyindo.

The accused was indicted for the murder of a woman he used to call 'mother'. The deceased used to return to the prison barracks where she lived with her husband. It was the prosecution case that on the material date, the accused escorted the deceased back home as was usual for him to do at about 8 p.m. and that he had murdered her on the way and removed from her some money. The court accepted the evidence that the accused was seen escorting the deceased at the material time and that he returned home drunk at about 11 p.m. There was no direct evidence as to what happened after that.

Held *inter alia*:

1. The case rested mainly on circumstantial evidence. As it was stated in *R v Taylor Wear, and Donovan* (1928) 21 Crim App Rep 20 quoted in *Tumuheirwe v Uganda* [1967] EA328. Circumstantial evidence is very often the best evidence. It is evidence of surrounding circumstances which, by intensified examination is capable of proving with the accuracy of mathematics. It is no derogation of evidence to say it is circumstantial.

2. However, circumstantial evidence had to be approached with caution because as was pointed out by Lord Normand in *Teper v R* [1952] AC 489. 'evidence

of this kind may be fabricated to cast suspicion on another ... It is also necessary before drawing the inference of the accused's guilt from circumstantial evidence to be sure that there are no other co-existing circumstances which would weaken or destroy the inference.'

CASE: *Uganda v Festo Bazze and another* Criminal Session Case No. 78/1972. The two accused were charged with murder under Section 183 of the Penal Code. The deceased was found dead in his house with several wounds on his body. The deceased's radio and bicycle were missing from the house. The bicycle was found in the house of A2. A2 told the the Chief that it was A1 who took the deceased's radio, after the deceased had been killed. A1 led the chief and other people to the place where the radio had been hidden.

Held *inter alia* that the circumstances of A1 being in possession of the deceased's radio pointed to no other reasonable conclusion than that he took part in killing the deceased unless he had explanation. Since he had no explanation to offer, he was convicted of murder.

Conclusion
It is to be noted that it is not only the fact of death that can be proved through circumstantial evidence. As will be discussed later, even other ingredients such as whether the accused was at the scene of the crime, the cause of death as well as the intention accompanying the homicide can all be based on circumstantial evidence. What is, however, important is what has been declared by courts such as in *Simon Musoke v R* 1958 EA715.

> In a case depending exclusively upon circumstantial evidence the court must, before deciding upon a conviction find that the inculpatory facts are incompatible with the innocence of the accused and incapable of explanation upon any other reasonable hypothesis than that of guilt.

Proof of fact of death by evidence of eyewitnesses
Uganda v John Ochieng [1992-93] HCB 80
CASE: The accused was indicted for murder. The prosecution relied on the evidence of three witnesses who saw and buried the body of the deceased to prove *inter alia*, the death of the deceased. All the three witnesses knew the deceased. No post mortem was tendered in evidence.

Held *inter alia*: Omission to tender a post-mortem examination report did not create any doubt that the deceased died, for death could be proved by evidence other than a medical report.

CASE: In *Uganda v Lazaro Daniel Idubale*, Criminal Session Case No. 84/95 (High Court)
Fact of death was proved through evidence of witnesses who saw the body of the deceased. Relied on *R v Chaya*; *Uganda v Iga* and held that though medical evidence is the best evidence to prove death and its cause, the same can still be proved to the requisite standard by evidence other than medical evidence.

Proof of fact of death by confession of the accused

CASE: *Uganda v Sebastiano Otti* [1994-95] HCB 21 (High Court of Uganda.), Justice Okello

The accused was indicted for murder. He admitted killing the deceased. In his defence, he claimed he shot the deceased with an arrow on information that somebody was stealing honey from his father's beehive. He claimed he acted in self defence as the deceased was armed with a panga. According to the prosecution, the deceased was shot in his own compound. No medical evidence was adduced to prove death.

Held *inter alia* that although there was no medical evidence to prove the deceased's death and its cause, death could still be proved beyond reasonable doubt by other cogent evidence in the absence of medical evidence. In the present case the accused himself admitted the death of the deceased.

Dead within a year and a day

According to Section 198 of the Uganda Penal Code, a person cannot be criminally responsible for the death of another (homicide), f the death does not occur within a year and a day of the accused's conduct/infliction of the injury. The rule restricts the right of the prosecution to prove that the assaulter caused death. In the words of the Penal Code:

> A person is not deemed to have killed another if the death of that person does not take place within a year and a day of the cause of death.

The rule is often justified on the ground that the purpose of criminal law is to prosecute but not to persecute. Consequently, a person who injures another should not remain indefinitely liable for a homicidal offence.

Death caused by unlawful act or omission

Before an accused can be convicted of any type of homicide, his/her conduct which led to the death must have been unlawful. What constitutes unlawfulness in homicide? We have already seen that there is a presumption that all homicides are unlawful. The unlawful conduct may be in form of an act or an omission.

Omission

An omission will constitute unlawful conduct only where the law imposes a duty to act. For example, a parent has a duty to her/his young child to save it from physical harm, to feed it. Section 6 of the Children Statute provides that it is the duty of every parent, guardian or person having custody of a child to maintain that child and, in particular that duty gives a child the right to:
1. Education and guidance
2. Immunisation
3. Adequate diet
4. Shelter
5. Medical attention.

We note that under Section 156 of the Uganda Penal Code, a person who deserts a child and thereby neglects his/her duty to maintain the child is guilty of a misdemeanour.[7]

And under Section 157, a parent or guardian who neglects to provide a child with necessities is guilty of a misdemeanour.[8] Consequently, if the parent refuses/neglects to feed the child and the child dies, the parent can be convicted of either murder or manslaughter, depending on the parent's state of mind. This would be because the failure/neglect or indeed the desertion would be an unlawful act in itself since the penal law has categorised such an act as unlawful and in fact punishable. The conduct would also be a violation of rights specifically created by the Children Statute. On the other hand, suppose an adult (A), stands at a road junction before crossing the road, and a young child (B) stands beside A waiting to cross the road. If A realises that B is going to cross the road at a moment when a fast moving car is approaching, but nevertheless does not hold the child back, although A is in position to do so, and B crosses the road and is in fact hit by the car, A has no criminal liability.

If a rich person (A) is aware that children in a child-headed household are without food but takes no steps to help them and in fact throws food that is excess in his/her house, and the children die of hunger, A is not guilty of any crime. Although A may be morally expected to 'save' the child's life, A has no legal duty to do so and can therefore not be penalised for inaction.

CASE: In the old English case of *Nicholls* (1874)13 Cox CC75 it was held that a person who voluntarily undertakes the care of another who is unable to care for himself owes a duty to that person. The undertaking of care may be done by some express (or overt) act, as in *Nicholls*, where D received into her home her young grandchild after the death of its mother. D was indicted for manslaughter by neglect. Brett directed the jury that:

> If a person chooses to undertake the care of a person who is helpless either from infancy, mental illness or other infirmity, he is bound to execute that responsibility and if (with the necessary *mens rea*) he allows him to die he is guilty of manslaughter.

Unlawful acts

In the majority of cases the conduct which constitutes part of the *actus reus*, the conduct which causes the homicide is an act as opposed to an omission. An act is the most common basis of criminal liability in homicides.

Use of excessive force amounts to unlawful conduct

Under Section 15 of the Penal Code, a person is entitled to use force to defend his/her person or property. Criminal law also entitles a person to use force in effecting an arrest.[9] However, under Section 16 of the Penal Code:

> Where any person is charged with a criminal offence arising out of the arrest, or attempted arrest, by him of a person who forcibly resists such arrest or attempts to evade being arrested, the court shall, in considering whether the means used were necessary, or the degree of force used was reasonable, for the apprehension of such person, have regard to the gravity of the offence which had been or was being committed by such person and the circumstances in which such offence had been or was being committed by such person.

And under Section 225 of the Penal Code:

> Any person authorised by law ... to use force is criminally responsible for any excess.

Thus where excessive force is used the conduct translates into an unlawful act.

CASE: *Uganda v Abdu Muherwa* [1972] EA 466
The accused was indicted for murder contrary to Section 183 of the Penal Code Act. It was the case for the prosecution that the accused waited in ambush to catch the thief who had been stealing his beans from the garden. When the deceased came and started uprooting the beans, the accused went and cut him with a panga on the left thigh severing major blood vessels which caused bleeding from which the deceased died. The accused made an alarm and neighbours who answered it found the deceased lying dead beside a bundle of beans. There were no marks of struggle at the scene. The accused admitted to those who answered the alarm that he had attacked and killed the deceased who had been a thief. At the trial the accused claimed that he had struggled with the deceased who had sustained the cut wound accidentally during the struggle. The prosecution contended that the accused had formed a prior intent to kill the deceased. It was contended on behalf of the accused that he was acting in self-defence.

Held *inter alia* that the accused was not acting in self-defence but he was merely arresting a thief of his beans who had annoyed him on a number of occasions when his beans had been stolen. The accused, like every citizen of Uganda, had the power, given to him by section 28 of the Criminal Procedure Code, to arrest a person found stealing, but he had exceeded that power by using excessive force and killing the deceased. This was clearly an unlawful act. The accused had thus caused the death of the deceased by an unlawful act.

CASE: *Marwa s/o Robi v R* [1959] EA 660
The court held that a person is entitled to use reasonable force to prevent the taking of his property. If in good faith, he uses more force than was reasonable and thereby kills the trespasser, the offence would amount to manslaughter.

Note: Use of excessive/unreasonable force constitutes the unlawfulness of the conduct. It turns what would otherwise be lawful protection of property, into an unlawful conduct. Where the force used is reasonable, the conduct is lawful and thus the homicide would be justifiable and not punishable.

CASE: *Uganda v Bugga* [1984] 10 (High Court)
The accused was charged with murder. After a dispute between the deceased and the accused, the deceased chased the accused and boxed him twice. The accused tried to escape from the deceased but he was hotly pursued by the deceased. In retaliation, the accused took a stick and hit the deceased ON the back of the head once. The deceased fell down and died.

The accused pleaded self defence.

Held: The accused did not retaliate with his bare hands but used a stick which he used with considerable force. The accused's retaliation was in excess of what was necessary to protect himself. The defence of self defence would therefore not be available. The defendant was found guilty of manslaughter.

CASE: *Sharmpal Singh s/o Pritam Singh v R* [1960] EA762
The appellant (accused) had been married to the deceased for less than one year. The evidence was that the marriage was a happy one. At the time of her death, the deceased was pregnant. The appellant was convicted of the murder of his wife by strangulation. The medical evidence against the appellant was that he had sexual intercourse with his wife just before her death. There were internal bruises to her neck and chest which could have been caused by pressure from an elbow or a knee on her chest and hands on her throat.

Discussion: What constituted the unlawful act?
Although the act of sexual intercourse with a wife does not constitute a crime, the appellant (accused) exceeded the amount of force allowed in a sexual act and thus conducted himself in an unlawful manner.

Note: Section 225 Penal Code:

> Any person authorised by law or by the consent of the person injured by him to use force is criminally responsible for any excess, according to the nature and quality of the act which constitutes the excess.

CASE: *Defasi Magayi v Uganda* [1965] EA 667. (East African Court of Appeal.)
The appellants were jointly tried and convicted of murder of a suspected thief whom they had beaten with sticks until he died. The beating was done in obedience to the order of a chief.

Held: On appeal it was held *inter alia* that none of the appellants could shelter behind the invitation or order of the chief, which they must have known was not a lawful order which they were bound to obey. In a judgement read by Sir Clement De Lestang, Justice of Appeal, it was *inter alia* said:

> It was contended on behalf of some of the appellants that since they went in answer to an alarm and behaved lawfully in assisting the chief to arrest the thieves and convey them to the chief's headquarters, they had no malice aforethought when in obedience to the chief they beat the deceased to death. We are unable to accept this contention. Although it is the custom in Uganda and elsewhere in East Africa to beat thieves the appellants cannot shelter behind the invitation or order of the chief. It was not a lawful order which they were bound to obey and they must have known as much. The fact that the chief said that he would 'face the case' is itself an indication that he and they knew that what they were doing was wrong.

> In conclusion we are satisfied that the appellants were properly convicted of murder and we dismiss the appeals.

CASE: *Kabengi v Uganda* [1978] HCB 216
The Court of Appeal for Uganda held *inter alia* that the use of excessive force in exercising the right of self defence renders the offence committed manslaughter.

CASE: In *George Kanalusasi v Uganda,* the accused was in his house at night when he was awakened by the barking of his dog. He went outside armed with a stick. He saw someone standing on the verandah and he promptly struck him with a stick. He thought that the fellow was a thief since night robberies were rampant in the area at that time. Although the stranger ran away, he collapsed in a nearby garden.

Held: The Supreme Court held that in the circumstances, the accused was entitled to strike the intruder in self defence. However, the force used was excessive (the use of a weapon on an unarmed person). The Supreme Court held that he was guilty of manslaughter.

Attempt to commit suicide an unlawful act
CASE: *Paulo s/o Mabula v R* [1953] 20 EACA 207
The appellant killed his wife. It was common ground that the deceased died as a result of a knife wound in her chest which she received while endeavouring to prevent the appellant from cutting his throat. The appellant contended that the injury was accidental, although it was argued by the prosecution that the appellant had intentionally injured the victim.

Held: The East African Court of Appeal found that where, as a result of an act by an accused intending to kill himself, another is killed, he is properly convicted of murder, even if he did not intend to kill that other person.

In the Court's judgement, it was pointed out that attempted suicide is a misdemeanour (and thus an unlawful act). Since the evidence before the court clearly established an intention to commit suicide by the appellant, the homicide which resulted from his conduct was unlawful and punishable.

Causation: Proof of cause of death
Before an accused is convicted of any homicide, it must be proved that it was his conduct that caused the death of the victim. It must be proved that there is a link between the death of the victim and the unlawful conduct of the accused. This must be proved beyond reasonable doubt. Thus the question is (i) what caused the death? (ii) who caused the death? In several cases, evidence may be adduced to the effect that the accused (A) injured the victim (B). We however need to realise that it is not all injuries that lead to death. Thus the prosecution must, in addition to proving that A injured B, prove that as a result of the said injuries, B died. It must be proved beyond reasonable doubt that it was the accused's injury that caused the death.

Where it is proved beyond reasonable doubt that the accused injured the deceased, but there is doubt as to whether it was the injury made by the accused which led to the death of the deceased, such accused person will be acquitted of either murder or manslaughter but can be convicted of either assault occasioning actual bodily harm (Section 236 Penal Code) or causing grievous bodily harm (Section 219 Penal Code), depending on the seriousness of the injuries occasioned. This is possible because the offences under sections 219 and 236 are minor and cognate offences of murder and manslaughter.

Causation: But what constitutes causation?
Contribution to death
By virtue of Section 196 of the Penal Code Act, responsibility for death can be attributed to a particular individual (the accused), even where his/her conduct was not the immediate or sole (only) cause of death. Even where the death resulted from a combination of the conduct of the accused *and* the conduct of either the victim or indeed a third party, an accused person can still be held responsible for the death.

The issue of causation is:
1. Factual
2. Legal

Factual cause
The doctrine of 'cause in fact' / factual causation investigates whether the killing of the victim is a product of the defendant's (accused's) act as tested by the principles of scientific causation. Two tests are applied:
1. The 'but-for' test
2. The 'substantial factor' test

The 'but-for' principle
The test answers the question whether the death can be attributed to the accused's conduct as a matter of fact. It must be shown that death was caused effectively by the accused. It must be proved that there is a direct 'link' between the accused's conduct and the death. According to Smith & Hogan (1992:333):

> D's act cannot be the cause of (death) if the (death) would have occurred in precisely the same way had D never done the act.

In other words, even if D had never acted as he had, death would have occurred in precisely the same way and at that particular time. It is this that scholars call the 'but-for' principle/test.

If in the absence of the accused's act, the victim would not have been killed, i.e. *but for* the accused's actions, the victim would still be alive, then the defendant's act is the actual/factual cause of the death. Application of this test indicates whether or not the death can be attributed to the accused's conduct as a matter of fact. The accused's action must be a *sine qua non* of the result. The but-for test resolves most ordinary homicide situations but is inadequate to resolve homicides which are a result of multiple actors.

The 'substantial factor' test
In addition to the 'but-for' test courts also consider whether the accused's act was a substantial factor in bringing about the death of the victim. This seems to mean that the accused's contribution must not be so minute that it will be ignored under the *de minimis* principle.[10] In the words of Card, Cross and Jones, 1992:194:

> The accused's conduct is not a factual cause of death unless the death would not have occurred, when and as it did, but for that conduct.

Card, Cross and Jones (1992:195) explains substantial cause thus: '… "substantial" in this context merely means that the accused's contribution to the death must be more than a minute or negligible contribution' (which would be ignored anyway under the general *de minimis* principle)

As Smith and Hogan (1992:334) put it 'killing is merely an acceleration of death and factors which produce a very trivial acceleration will be ignored.'

Perkins and Boyce, *Criminal Law* (3rd ed.) provides a clear example:

> '… suppose one wound severed the jugular vein whereas the other barely broke the skin of the hand, and as the life blood gushed from the victim's neck, one drop oozed from the bruise on his finger … metaphysicians will conclude that the extra drop of lost blood hastened the end by the infinitesimal fraction of a second. But the law will apply the *substantial factor* test and for juridical purposes the death will be imputed only to the severe injury … [cited in Smith & Hogan, 1992:335].

In some cases the courts have used the term 'significant contribution to death' rather than 'substantial cause of death', but there is no difference between the effects of the two terms.

Intervening Acts or Events (novus actus *or* nova causa *interveniens)*

Difficulty may arise where an accused inflicts an injury on the victim but before the victim's death, some other act or event occurs to the victim, who then dies. (i.e. something else occurs aside from the conduct of the accused, something which might also be considered a cause of the death). Sometimes a new act or event may break the chain of causation and relieve the accused of responsibility. Such event will have broken the causal connection between the accused's conduct and the subsequent happening (i.e. the death) and therefore relieves him/her of criminal responsibility for such death.

It is not, however, every intervening act or omission of a causal nature that will relieve the accused from liability for the subsequent death. An intervening act of a third party may end an accused's criminal liability only if the intervening act is the sole cause of the harm.

In general, the issue of whether or not the first 'assaulter' is relieved of responsibility boils down to a question of remoteness: was the conduct of the first 'assaulter' too remote from the eventual harm (death) to justify imputing responsibility to her/him?

We can safely say that to constitute a *novus actus,* the intervening cause must be something that is extremely abnormal and unexpected. And if done by another person, it must be done voluntarily. Some courts have held that anything which might be considered a natural event does not disturb the causal link between the conduct of the accused and the consequence (as long as the natural event was not sufficiently abnormal).

How is causation proved?

The cause of death, both *who* caused it and *what* caused it can be proved in any of the following ways:

1. Plea of guilty by the accused. (Admission/confession by the accused)

2. The cause of death may be proved conclusively by an autopsy/medical evidence.
3. Evidence of eyewitnesses
4. Circumstantial evidence

What is important is that the issue, i.e. the cause of death, is proved beyond reasonable doubt and that the accused is properly linked to the death.

Who and what caused the death: Admission by the accused

There is no law which prohibits the court from convicting an accused of a homicidal event, based on the accused's own admission that he caused the death of the victim.

Thus in *Mwanje Yoweri v Uganda* Criminal Appeal No. 39/1999, the Court of Appeal held *inter alia* that a plea of guilty summarily puts the accused's criminal liability beyond doubt.

CASE: In *Rex v Kinanda Bin Mwaisumo*, the deceased before his death gave the name of another man as his assailant and that another man, (Mapumba) was arrested and charged with murder. Up till then the prosecution had no evidence whatsoever to connect the accused (Kinanda Bin Mwaisumo) with the crime and if he had been content to keep silent and allow the case against Mapumba to proceed to its conclusion, it seems probable that he would never have even been suspected. However, Kinanda went to the authorities and explained that the deceased, owing to darkness, had made a mistake as to who his assailant was; that he, the accused (Kinanda) had killed the deceased and that, rather than let an innocent man suffer, he was prepared to take the consequences himself. As a result, Mapumba was released and Kinanda was charged. The Court of Appeal for Eastern Africa held *inter alia* that should an accused person incriminate himself he may be convicted even though the evidence at the close of the crown case is insufficient to warrant a conviction.

CASE: *Chacha s/o Wamburu* 20 EACA 339

The Court of Appeal for Eastern Africa held *inter alia* that there is no general rule either of law or practice that a plea of guilty should not be accepted from an African in a capital case; but precautions are necessary.

In its judgement the Court went on to state that where counsel appeared for the accused, the judge may be entitled, if the plea is unequivocal in terms, to accept counsel's assurance that he has advised his client fully as to the elements of the offence charged and the nature and consequences of a plea of guilty, and thereupon to accept the plea; but it may well be a wiser practice to examine the accused himself in the way suggested in Yonasani's case (*Yonasani Egalu and Others*, 9 EACA 65)

Conclusion: Where an accused pleads guilty in a capital offence:
1. The court must be certain that the accused's plea is unequivocal to every element/ingredient of the offence.
2. It is wise that caution is taken even when the accused is represented by counsel.

What is important therefore is that the accused is unequivocally pleading to each ingredient of the offence.

CASE: *Rex v Changuony Arap Kisang* Criminal Appeal No.148/1946
On being charged with murder, the accused stated 'it is true I killed her because she had bewitched me ... I understand that my words may be taken as a plea of guilty to murder'

The accused was convicted of murder on his own plea. On appeal, it was held by the Court of Appeal for Eastern Africa:

> That as there is no statutory provision invalidating a plea of guilty to a charge of murder it was in no sense improper in the circumstances of this case for a Judge to convict on such a plea.

Who and what caused the death: Proof by autopsy/medical evidence

CASE: *Uganda versus Sepiriya Makayi & Others,* Criminal Session Case No. 290/1997
It was held by Acting Justice Maniraguha that 'considering the law it is accepted that the cause of death may be proved conclusively by the findings of a doctor through an autopsy. But where it is not performed or is at variance with other available evidence then court can rely on the evidence of the eye witnesses.'

CASE: *Bumakali Lutwama & 5 Others v Uganda* Supreme Court Appeal No. 38/1989.
The court rejected the doctors' report because the injuries depicted therein were different from those seen by eye witnesses, so the doctor seemed to have examined a different body.

In effect there was no post mortem report regarding the particular deceased. The Supreme Court relied on the evidence of eye witnesses who saw the body of the deceased and the number of wounds on it. It was concluded from the severity of the wounds and the fact that the deceased's body had the hands tied with banana leaves that this evidence proved both the death and the cause of the same.

CASE: *Siraj Sajjabi v Uganda* Criminal Appeal No.31 of 1989 (Supreme Court of Uganda
The appellant was convicted of the murder of the deceased. The prosecution case was that the appellant shot the deceased in the head with a pistol. The deceased fell down and died on the spot. The deceased's body was taken to Mulago hospital on the day of the incident for post-mortem examination. However, no evidence was led by the prosecution as to whether the post-mortem examination was carried out and if so, with what result. The trial judge was not bothered by that omission as he was satisfied that the deceased died of the gun-shot injury on his head.

Held on appeal:

> that there can be no doubt that the cause of death was the gun shots, since the deceased was well and in good health until he was shot and died almost instantly. Be that as it may ... the trial court should have called the medical evidence as to the cause of death since it was available.

The court relied on the evidence of eyewitnesses to hold that the deceased died of gun shots. Thus the absence of a post mortem report is not necessarily fatal to the prosecution case.

Who and what caused the death: Evidence of eyewitnesses

CASE: *Republic v Cheya and Another* [1973] EA 500

The two accused assaulted and tried to remove the deceased from a group of women at a dance because they objected to his behaviour. Other people joined in and assaulted the deceased who later died.

At the trial of the accused for murder no post-mortem report was produced and the prosecution relied on the evidence of eye-witnesses to establish the death of the deceased and its cause. For the accused it was contended that there was no common intention of the mob and no proof that any blow inflicted by the accused caused the death of the deceased.

The post mortem report which the prosecution sought to introduce in evidence, was for the purposes of proving:

1. That the victim was in fact dead.
2. That his death was caused by the accused was ruled inadmissible because the post mortem report was not signed by whoever prepared it, and secondly the qualifications of whoever prepared it were not shown on the report ....

Held: *inter alia* that: the fact of death and the cause of it could be established otherwise than by medical evidence.

> However the absence of medical evidence as to death and the cause of it are not fatal. ... it is open to the prosecution to produce and rely on other evidence to establish [the fact of death and its cause]. Such other evidence can be testimonies of witnesses, witnesses who not only saw the deceased being (viciously) assaulted but saw him at the hospital and later his dead body. It was testified that they saw the deceased viciously assaulted and injured, that he was bleeding in several places, he was admitted in hospital with these injuries and that he died one or two days later.

See also *Uganda v Natseba Lawrence, Mushikama Watete & Others* Criminal Session Case No. 283/97 (High Court)

In this case even if the post mortem report was disregarded by the court, the cause of death was proved through the testimony of eye-witnesses who saw the deceased being cut twice on the head with a panga after which she collapsed and died shortly thereafter.

CASE: *Uganda v Geofrey Saaku* Criminal Case 112/97

The accused was indicted for the murder of D1 and D2, contrary to Sections 183 and 184 of the Penal Code. The prosecution called two witnesses PW1 and PW2. PW1 testified that on the night of 5/07/92, she was inside the house with D1 and D2. She heard somebody asking D1 (her grandmother) to come out of the house and receive a gift. D1 went to the door where the caller was calling from, while carrying D2 on her back. D1 also carried a lamp with her. The caller (accused) handed D1 a jerrycan containing fuel. The jerrycan burst, caught fire when it got in contact with the lamp. D1 raised an alarm saying that the accused had burnt them. The accused ran away.

The bodies of D1 and D2 were burnt beyond recognition. PW2 took them to Mu go. Both deceased persons died on the same day. They were buried. The police dia not visit the scene but the LCs and local chiefs of the area came.

The defence submitted that there was no evidence by the prosecution to prove the cause of death. What was on record was that the deceased were burnt by fire which came from the jerrycan after being attracted by the lamp. There was no evidence to show that there was petrol. No evidence from an expert was brought to that effect.

Judgement:

It is true no medical evidence was adduced from the medical department and no evidence was adduced from an expert to show that it was petrol from the jerrican which came into contact with the candle which turned into an inferno that burnt the two deceased. There was however evidence of an eye witness to the cause of death (PW1). She saw the two catch fire and eventually both of them died as a result of explosive from the jerrican. There is also the evidence of PW2 who took the deceased to Mulago Hospital.

The law is that the fact of death and cause of it could be established otherwise than by medical evidence. [See *Republic v Cheeye* 1973, EA 500, *Yozefu Kyebanda* 1972 2 ULR 19, *Uganda v Hussein Duka* 1982 HCB 89]. The evidence of PW1 & PW2 establish the fact and cause of death therefore mere absence of medical evidence as to death and cause of it is not necessarily fatal since there is other reliable and satisfactory evidence to that effect.

Notes: The fact of death and the cause of death can be established otherwise than by medical evidence.

Who and what caused the death: Circumstantial evidence

CASE: *Charles Rwamunda v Uganda* Criminal Appeal No.6/93. (Supreme Court)
It was held *inter alia* that circumstantial evidence can adequately link an accused to a homicide. To prove the case beyond reasonable doubt, the prosecution must satisfy the court to the effect that the inculpatory facts pointed to the accused as having been the only person who could have committed the crime, and must not be capable of explanation on any other hypothesis, other than the guilt of the appellant.
See p.26 for details of the case.

CASE: *James Kiyingi Munanga, John Fisher Iga, John Bosco Kiwanuka v Uganda,*Criminal Appeal No. 10/1993
The Supreme Court of Uganda confirmed a verdict of guilty of murder based on circumstantial evidence. The verdict was based on circumstantial evidence since no person witnessed the killing of the deceased by the accused persons.

Accused 2 and Accused 3 shared a room in a certain house. The deceased lived in the same house but in a separate room. The body of the deceased was found on a footpath. In A1's house nearby, the police found bloodstained clothes. When A2 and A3's room was searched other bloodstained clothes were discovered. The investigating officer scooped some bloodstained soil from where the body of the deceased was found and conveyed it together with the blood stained clothes found in the premises of the accused, to the government chemist for analysis. At the trial, the chemist's report was tendered and it was said that the bloodstains found on the soil and on the clothes found in the accused's premises all belonged to group O, i.e. the blood stains on the items recovered from the appellants' houses belonged to the same group as the blood of the deceased. The appellants were arrested and charged with murder. On the day of the murder, the three men disappeared from the village.

The Supreme Court said inter alia that:

> Circumstantial evidence is evidence of surrounding circumstances which, by undersigned coincidences is capable of proving facts in issue accurately; it is no derogation of evidence to say that it is circumstantial evidence. However, circumstantial evidence must always be narrowly examined only because evidence of this kind may be fabricated to cast suspicion on another. It is, therefore, necessary before drawing the inference of the accused's guilt from circumstantial evidence to be sure that there are no other co-existing circumstances which would weaken or destroy the inference.

Who and what caused the death: Confession by accused and circumstantial evidence

CASE: *Uganda v Festo Bazze & Another.* Criminal Session Case No. 78/1972. Before Chief Justice Kiwanuka.

The two accused persons were charged with murder of the deceased contrary to Section 183 of the Penal Code. The deceased was found dead in his house with several wounds on his body.

Deceased's radio and bicycle were missing from the house. A2 later confessed to the chief that he had taken part in killing the deceased. He said he had been hired to kill the deceased by the deceased's son, A1. The chief asked A2 where the deceased's property was. A2 led the chief to his house where the bicycle was found. The chief also found 4 boxes of matches in a packet, and a wet shirt on which he found what looked to have been blood stains recently washed. A2 told the chief that the deceased's radio was taken by A1. Later A1 led the chief and some other people to a place where the radio was hidden – in the bush, wrapped in a gunny bag. At the trial the two accused denied having murdered the deceased.

1. The circumstances of A1 being in possession of deceased's radio hidden in the bush pointed to no other reasonable conclusion than that he took part in killing the deceased unless he had explanation. He had no explanation to offer.
2. A2's confession would have sufficed to warrant his conviction. But there was the finding of the bicycle in his possession as well as matches in his house. Those two pieces of evidence constituted yet another basis for his being found guilty.

Held: Both accused were found guilty of murder.

See also *Uganda v Albino Ajok.*

What caused the death: Linking the death to the accused's assault

It must be proved beyond reasonable doubt that it is the accused's act which led to the death of the deceased. Any doubt as to the cause of death works in favour of the accused.

CASE: *Gichunge vs R* [1972] EA 546
The appellant stabbed the deceased in the chest causing a collapse of the left lung. The victim was admitted to hospital and later discharged. Thirty-six days after being wounded, and 15 days after being discharged from hospital, the victim died. According to a doctor's report, the victim's 'death was due to pneumonia and tetanus following a stabbing injury to the chest.' The doctor's report as to the cause of death was admitted without the doctor being called as a witness since he had left the country. Gichunge was convicted of murder but appealed.

Issue: Whether the stab wound was the cause of death.

Held:

1. In view of the possibility that death had been caused by an intervening circumstance, it had not been proved that death was caused by the appellant.
2. Unlawfully causing grievous harm is a complete minor offense in relation to murder.

In the judgement of the court it was *inter alia* said:

> … As Mngai (the deceased) died 36 days after being wounded, and 15 days after being discharged from hospital, as death had not occurred immediately after being wounded, it was of the greatest importance that there should be evidence linking the cause of death (that is to say tetanus and pneumonia) with the stab wound, if the appellant was to be held responsible for the death. As to this, there is the doctor's report that 'death was due to pneumonia and tetanus following a stabbing injury to the chest.'

> So far as this statement is considered as an expression of fact, it is correct. The pneumonia and tetanus followed, in point of time, the stabbing. But there is absolutely no evidence, anywhere in the record, that the pneumonia and tetanus were a direct result and consequence of the stabbing. It is most likely that they were, but we cannot exclude the possibility that, had he been cross-examined, Dr Knights might have conceded the possibility that the pneumonia and tetanus supervened independently of the stabbing, in which case the appellant would not be responsible for the death.

> … [There was a] lacuna in the prosecution case, that is to say, the link between the cause of death and the injury inflicted by the appellant. This lacuna could only have been filled, in the absence of Dr. Knights, (he had left the country), and by calling as a witness another medical expert, [T] he possibility of death having been caused by some intervening circumstance, unconnected with the stabbing, had not been excluded in this case. We accordingly set aside the conviction for murder.

> We were satisfied beyond reasonable doubt that it was the appellant who stabbed the deceased, and we accordingly convicted him of unlawfully doing grievous harm.

CASE: *Kamanzi Fred v Uganda* Criminal Appeal No.14/97. (Supreme Court)
On 4/09/92 the appellant who was leading a gang of attackers broke into the house of the deceased and cut the deceased with a panga on his head. The appellant was arrested at the scene of the crime. The deceased was taken to hospital, admitted and treated. He was discharged but about a month later he died at his home.

According to the post mortem report, 'the body of the deceased had a cut wound on the scalp, measuring 4 cm long, 3 cm deep and 1 cm wide. Bloody pus discharged from nose and mouth. Cause of death and reasons – internal haemorrhage complicating into infection.' The trial judge entered a guilty verdict for murder and the Court of Appeal upheld the trial court's decision.

One of the grounds of appeal to the Supreme Court was that the prosecution did not discharge the burden of proof beyond reasonable doubt that the injury sustained by the deceased on 4/09/92 was the direct cause of death on 8/10/92.

Held:
1. The medical report did not establish beyond reasonable doubt that the deceased died as a result of the cut wound inflicted by the appellant. It was not clearly established beyond reasonable doubt by either medical evidence or other evidence that the external wound on the deceased's scalp was the direct and immediate cause of 'the internal haemorrhage complicating into infection' which caused the death.
2. There was a lacuna in the prosecution evidence as to whether the internal haemorrhage complicating into infection resulted from the scalp cut wound inflicted by the appellant or by another cause wholly unconnected with the injury. The onus was on the prosecution to prove beyond reasonable doubt that the infection seen by the doctor had resulted from the cut wound sustained by the deceased when he was cut by the appellant. If the doctor who had performed the post mortem had been summoned to testify he would have established whether or not the internal haemorrhage which complicated into infection resulted from that cut wound inflicted by the appellant or whether the infection resulted from other causes. The doctor should have been called to elaborate on the medical evidence as to the cause of death.
3. The cause of death was described by the post mortem report as 'internal haemorrhage complicating into infection'. There was a question left unanswered by the report: Was it the cut wound which caused the internal haemorrhage complicating into infection?
4. The onus was on the prosecution to rule out any possibility of deceased's death having come about by some other circumstances wholly unconnected with the injury inflicted by the appellant. In our view the Court of Appeal erred to say they were unable to say that some other causes intervened when the prosecution had failed to prove beyond reasonable doubt that the cause of death followed directly from the wound inflicted by the appellant.

Concluding remark: It is not enough to establish that an accused caused an injury. Prosecution must also prove that that very injury and not any other cause led to the death of the deceased.

CASE: *Fred Sabahashi v Uganda* Criminal Appeal No.23/1993 (Supreme Court of Uganda)

The appellant Fred Sabahashi was jointly indicted with John Kizza of murder under Section 183. They were both convicted of manslaughter under Section 182. Sabahashi appealed against the conviction.

Facts: The appellant was a Local Administration Askari. On 27/07/90, the deceased and another were arrested for theft of money. They were brought by a group of people to the sub-county chief, to whom they admitted having stolen the money. The chief handed them over to the appellant for detention. After a short while, the appellant and Kizza started beating the suspects with sticks and kicking them with boots. PW4 and PW5 witnessed the assault and advised the appellant and Kizza, to stop torturing the suspects.

In the evening, when the officer in charge of the station went to check on the suspects in their detention cell, he found the deceased groaning and kicking his legs. He went to his rescue but found him dead. Although the doctor did not open up the body, he examined it and recorded that the body had several abrasions and bruises all over. He formed the opinion that the cause of death was fracture of the skull.

The appellant appealed against the conviction inter alia on the grounds that there was no proof that it was the appellant who had caused the fatal blow and that there was no proof of common intention between the appellant and Kizza.

The Supreme Court **held** *inter alia* that:

... It is true that none of the witnesses identified which of the two accused persons struck the fatal blow. But there was no evidence that the deceased was assaulted on the head at the time of his arrest or later in the cells after the torture by the accused persons which had been witnesses by the prosecution witnesses. The appellant and his co-accused had been seen engaged in the unlawful act of torturing the deceased who was lying down by beating and kicking him interchangeably. It could be inferred from their actions that they had shared a common intention to prosecute an unlawful purpose which resulted in the death of the deceased. If they shared a common intention then each of them would be guilty of the offence irrespective of which of them struck the fatal blow.

From the appellant's presence and active participation in assaulting the deceased and his failure to disassociate himself from the actions of his co-accused Kizza, it was reasonable to infer that the two had formed a common intention to prosecute an unlawful purpose which was to torture and assault a self confessed thief who was in their custody. Each of the accused was liable for the fatal blow which caused the deceased's death. It is no answer to plead that it was not established as to which of them inflicted that fatal blow, for each of them is deemed to have committed the offence, once they had common intention.

CASE: *Yowanna Lubowa v R.* Criminal Appeal No.55/1953 (Court of Appeal for Eastern Africa)

The appellant was convicted of murder. No evidence was led as to the time and date of the deceased's death in hospital.

Held: In cases of homicide, where a person dies in hospital following an attack upon him causing his death, evidence should always be given as to the deceased's admission to hospital, the treatment given him therein and the date and time of his death.

CASE: *Uganda v Mohamed Tembo and Others* [1992- 1993] HCB 78

The accused persons were indicted for murder of the deceased. Prosecution alleged that the accused persons with others in a crowd beat up the deceased with sticks and a piece of rubber from a motor tyre. They were armed also with pangas and knives. The accused beat her because they said she had bewitched the first accused's wife who also died that day.

A post mortem was not done on the deceased, but she was buried with the permission of the police.

Held *inter alia*: In murder cases, the cause of death must be established. In the absence of an autopsy, circumstantial evidence may be used. In this case, however, though the accused were armed with lethal weapons, the size and nature of the wounds were not described. Not all cut wounds lead to death. It is therefore unsafe to conclude that the injuries sustained in the violence were the cause of her death, and therefore conviction for murder or manslaughter could not be secured.

Accused found guilty of assault occasioning actual bodily harm.

Notes:
- The cause of death can be proved through circumstantial evidence.
- Absence of a post mortem report is not fatal to the prosecution case.
- The cause of death must be established beyond reasonable doubt.
- Not all cut wounds lead to death, it is not enough for the prosecution to prove that an accused caused injuries to the victim; it must be proved that the injuries in question led to death.

CASE: *Anyangu and Others v Republic* [1968] EA239 Court of Appeal for East Africa.

A gang of burglars armed with offensive weapons broke into the house of one Nifa. They used violence towards Nifa and her daughter and in the words of the trial judge 'stripped the house of all its portable contents'. The two women raised an alarm and two men came to assist. These two men came upon the gang near the gate of Nifa's compound and were attacked by the gang. One managed to escape but the other was struck with pangas and sticks and killed. The four appellants were convicted of murder. They appealed against their convictions.

Held *inter alia*:

> The evidence did not establish who inflicted the fatal injury on the deceased or who took part in the assault on him. The learned trial judge correctly directed himself that in these circumstances the members of the gang could be convicted of murder only if Section 21 of the Penal Code applied, that is to say, that the commission of murder was a probable consequence of the prosecution of the common purpose of the gang which was clearly burglary. Having regard to the fact that the gang was armed with pangas, a hammer, sticks and torches and that violence was actually used he concluded that the killing was a probable consequence of the burglarious expedition and that Section 21 applied. With this conclusion we agree.

CASE: *Charles Rwamunda v Uganda* Supreme Court, Criminal Appeal No.6/93

The appellant was convicted of manslaughter contrary to Section 182 of the Uganda

Penal Code by the High Court. The victim in the case died almost a month after the incident (an assault which caused injuries). In concluding that death was caused by the appellant, the High Court based its decision on circumstantial evidence. The appellant appealed. The first ground of the appeal was that the cause of death of the victim had not been proved beyond reasonable doubt.

Counsel for the appellant argued that there was a lapse of time from the incident to the death and there was no evidence which explained what had happened during this interval. It was also noted that the panga exhibited in court as the homicidal weapon was not identified beyond reasonable doubt by the prosecution witnesses. According to the doctor's report, the cause of death was due to raised intracranial haemorrhage, caused by an abscess formation in the sagittal sinus.

Furthermore, the weapon was not tested by the Government Chemist so as to confirm that it had the same blood grouping as the victim. It therefore was not known what weapon was used.

In reaction to the ground of appeal, the Supreme Court said:

1. It must be the invariable practice for the prosecution and court to show the alleged murder weapon to the Doctor, for his opinion to be recorded whether it is or is not consistent with the wounds on the deceased, if the weapon is accepted as such by the court.
2. Where death does not occur immediately after an attack, it is important to ascertain whether there has been a break in the chain of causation. It is necessary to ascertain whether there has been any intervention, exculpating the accused person.

Notes:

1. The fact and cause of death can be proved through evidence of eye witnesses.
2. Absence of medical evidence as to the fact of death and as to its cause is not necessarily fatal to the prosecution case, as long as there is other reliable evidence to the effect.
3. Homicide, unless accidental, is always unlawful except when excusable.

Proof of death and proof of causation: Absence of medical evidence

In *Uganda v Richard Kadidi alias Kabagambe* [1992-93] HCB 59 Justice Karokora held, *inter alia* that although there was no post mortem report, it is now trite law that death can be proved without medical evidence.

Nevertheless in *Richard Munnube v Uganda* Criminal Appeal No.15/1984, the Supreme Court expressed the view that, medical evidence should always be adduced if available as in homicide cases the cause of death must be established and it is unsafe to rely on allegations by lay men as the cause of death.

Proof of cause of death: report by a clinical officer

CASE: *Uganda v Bagadya David* Criminal Session Case 312/99 (High Court)
Where a clinical officer is called upon to perform a post mortem examination, the prosecution must establish that he was competent to carry out the examination.

Proof of cause of death: Conclusion

CASE: *Richard Munnu v Uganda* Criminal Appeal No. 15/84

Although as seen in several cases courts have declared that absence of medical evidence is not fatal to the prosecution case if the cause of death can be proved through other ways, in this case the Supreme Court stated that:

> In our view, medical evidence should always be adduced if available as in homicide cases the cause of death must be established and it is unsafe to rely on allegations by lay men as to the cause of death.

Contributing causes in homicide

The principles of Legal Attribution are dealt with by Section 196 of the Uganda Penal Code which clearly states that the accused need not be the sole or the main cause of death. What is important is that the accused's contribution must not be so minute or negligible that it will be ignored under the *de minimis* principle.[11] If the accused's conduct is proved to have been a substantial factor in a death, the accused can still be responsible for the death even if his/her conduct would not on its own have caused death.

According to Section 196: A person is deemed to have caused the death of another person, although his act is not the immediate or sole cause of death in any of the following cases:

a) If he or she inflicts bodily injury on another person in consequence of which that person undergoes surgical or medical treatment which causes death. In this case it is immaterial whether the treatment was proper or mistaken, if it was employed in good faith and with common knowledge and skill, but the person inflicting the injury is not deemed to have caused the death if the treatment which was its immediate cause was not employed in good faith or was so employed without common knowledge or skill.

b) If he or she inflicts a bodily injury on another which would not have caused death if the injured person had submitted to proper surgical or medical treatment or had observed the proper precautions as to his or her mode of living.

c) If by actual or threatened violence he or she causes such other person to perform an act which causes the death of such person, such act being a means of avoiding such violence which in the circumstances would appear natural to the person whose death is so caused.

d) If by any act or omission he or she hastened the death of a person suffering under any disease or injury which apart from such act or omission would have caused death.

e) If his or her act or omission would not have caused death unless it had been accompanied by an act or omission of the person killed or of other persons.

Section 196 (a) Uganda Penal Code: Presumption that medical doctor acts in good faith

Under Section 196 (a) the law assumes that when a qualified medical doctor treats an injured person, the doctor acts in good faith. It is also assumed that the doctor employs knowledge and skill.

It is also noted that under Section 224 of the Penal Code Act:

a person is not criminally responsible for performing in good faith and with reasonable care and skill a surgical operation upon any person for his benefit ... if the performance of the operation is reasonable, having regard to the patient's state at the time, and to all the circumstances of the case.

Consequently if an accused (A) injures another person (V) and V goes through a surgical operation or is subjected to any other medical treatment which then leads to his/her death, A would still be responsible for V's death, unless it is proved that the doctor acted in bad faith or without knowledge.

CASE: *Rex v Njarura s/o Ndugo,* Criminal Appeal 223/1943 (East African Court of Appeal)
The deceased received a wound which was not of itself dangerous, but the deceased, who suffered from fatty degeneration of the heart, died under an anaesthetic administered for the purpose of stitching the wound. The medical evidence was that all usual precautions were taken before the anaesthetic was administered. It was subsequently discovered that the deceased suffered from fatty degeneration of the heart, as a result of which he died of heart failure under the anaesthetic. The doctor who carried out the operation said '... Death was due to I consider heart failure. If he had not been given the anaesthetic he would not have died. It is quite possible that he would have lived had he not been operated on ... I took the usual precautions before administering the anaesthetic.'
   The first ground of appeal against conviction was that, assuming the appellant to be legally responsible for the wound, he was not legally responsible for the death, because the treatment which was the immediate cause of the death was not proved to have been 'employed in good faith' or was 'employed without common knowledge or skill'.
   Counsel for the appellant argued that treatment cannot be said to have been 'employed in good faith' unless it was advisable or necessary, and that it was for the prosecution to establish affirmatively that in this case the operation and the administration of a general anaesthetic were advisable and necessary.

Held by the East African Court of Appeal:

That, in the absence of any evidence to the contrary, the court of trial was justified in presuming that a qualified medical practitioner would not perform an operation unless it was in his opinion necessary or advisable.

CASE: *R v Mwagambosho Gishodi* 8 EACA 28
The appellant inflicted two deep and serious wounds upon the deceased, who died as a result of sepsis from these wounds. The wounds had been stitched by a medical dresser. The medical evidence was to the effect that the wounds should have been drained instead of being stitched, but even if they had been drained, there would still have been a risk of sepsis setting in.

Held: What the dresser did was not unreasonable in the circumstances, and did not relieve the appellant of responsibility for causing death.

CASE: *R v Jordan* (1956) 40 Crim App Rep 152

The court of Criminal Appeal quashed a conviction for murder on a charge of causing death by stabbing after taking the exceptional step of admitting fresh medical evidence. This evidence went to show that death was not caused by the injury but by negligent medical treatment. The stab wound had pierced the intestine, but this was mainly healed at the time of death. The immediate cause of death was pneumonia produced by the administration of an antibiotic, to which the deceased was shown to be intolerant, and the intravenous introduction of wholly abnormal quantities of liquid. Both treatments were stated to be palpably wrong by medical witnesses.

Conclusion

A person inflicting the injury is not responsible for the death if the treatment was not employed in good faith or was employed without common knowledge or skill.

Section 196 (b) Uganda Penal Code: The effect of neglect by the injured person

The common law rule is that neglect or maltreatment by the injured person does not in itself exempt the assaulter from liability for the ultimate death.

CASE: *Walls'* case (1802)28 State Tr. 51 (cited in Smith and Hogan, 1992: 343)

The accused was convicted of the murder of a man by the illegal infliction on him of a flogging of 800 lashes. There was evidence that the victim had aggravated his condition by drinking spirits. The jury were told:

> … there is no apology for a man if he puts another in so dangerous and hazardous a situation by his treatment of him, that some degree of unskilfulness and mistaken treatment of himself may possibly accelerate the fatal catastrophe. One man is not at liberty to put another into such perilous circumstances as these, and to make it depend upon his own prudence, knowledge, skill or experience what may hurry on or complete that catastrophe, or on the other hand may render him service.

CASE: *Holland* (1841) 2 Mood and R 351 (cited in Smith and Hogan 1992: 343).

D waylaid and assaulted P, cutting him severely across one of his fingers with an iron instrument. P refused to follow the surgeon's advice to have the finger amputated, although he was told that if he did not, his life would be in great danger. The wound caused lockjaw [tetanus], the finger was then amputated, but it was too late and P died of lockjaw. The surgeon's evidence was that if the finger had been amputated at first, P's life could probably have been saved. Justice Maule told the jury that it made no difference whether the wound was in its own nature instantly mortal, or whether it became the cause of death by reason of the deceased not having adopted the best mode of treatment. The question was whether, in the end, the wound inflicted by the prisoner was the real cause of death.

Holland was followed in *Blaue.*

CASE: *Blaue* [1975]3 All ER 446

D stabbed P, a young girl, and pierced her lung. She was told that she would die if she did not have a blood transfusion. Being a Jehovah's witness, she refused on religious grounds. She died from the bleeding caused by the wound. D was convicted of manslaughter and argued that P's refusal to have a blood transfusion, being unreasonable, had broken the chain of causation. It was held that the judge had rightly instructed the jury that the wound was a cause of death.

Lord Justice Lawton said:

> It has long been the policy of the law that those who use violence on other people must take their victims as they find them. This in our judgement means the whole man, not just the physical man. It does not lie in the mouth of the assailant to say that his victim's religious beliefs, which inhibited him from accepting certain kinds of treatment, were unreasonable. The question for decision is what caused the death. The answer is the stab wound.

CASE: *Kamanzi Fred v Uganda* Supreme Court, Criminal Appeal No.14/97
On 4/09/92 the appellant broke into the house of the deceased and cut him with a panga on his head. The deceased was taken to hospital and was discharged. On 8/10/92 (close to a month after the attack) he died. According to the doctor's report, death was caused by internal haemorrhage complicating into infection.

The appellant was convicted of murder by the High Court. His appeal to the court of Appeal was dismissed. He appealed to the Supreme Court.

One of the grounds of appeal was that the lower courts erred in law and fact when they held that the appellant caused the death of the victim.

Held: The Supreme Court held:
1. It is not enough for the prosecution to establish that the accused inflicted an injury on the deceased. Prosecution must prove that it was that injury that caused the death and not any other case unconnected with the accused's injury. It must prove that deceased died as a direct result of the cut wound inflicted by the accused. It must be established that the external wound on the deceased's scalp was the direct cause of 'the internal haemorrhage complicating into infection' which caused the death. This is because an intervening cause unconnected with the original cause breaks the chain of causation.
2. The prosecution should call the doctor who performed the post mortem to establish whether or not the internal haemorrhage which complicated into infection resulted from the cut wound inflicted on the deceased's scalp or whether the infection resulted from other causes.

Prosecution counsel submitted that Section 189(b)[12] was applicable to the facts but the Supreme Court disagreed with the contention and said:

> ...if the appellant inflicted the cut wound on deceased's head and then that cut wound was the cause of death or if that cut wound caused the internal haemorrhage which caused death, this cut wound would be the direct cause. Therefore, Section 189(b) would not be relevant if the cut wound was the direct cause of death.

> The cause of death was described in Exh P1 (Post mortem report) as 'internal haemorrhage

complicating into infection'. There was a question left unanswered by that Exh.: Was it the cut wound which caused the internal haemorrhage complicating into infection?

Having held that the death had come about as a direct result of the cut wound, we were baffled to see the Justices of Appeal holding that Section 189(b) applied to the facts. There was no medical evidence on record to prove that the injury would not have caused death if the deceased had submitted to proper surgical medical treatment or had observed proper precaution as to his mode of living.

The appellant was convicted under Section 209(a) of the Penal Code[13] as guilty of grievous harm.

CASE: *Tindigwihura Mbahe v Uganda* Criminal Appeal No. 9/1987. (Supreme Court) The appellant attacked and injured the deceased. According to the doctor's report, death was caused by massive bleeding from the vessels.

The appellant was convicted of murder and sentenced to death by the High Court. He appealed against the conviction. It was contended by the defence at the appellant's trial that the deceased died due to negligence by his relatives because they did not take her to the hospital for medical treatment. The trial judge as well as the Supreme Court rejected the contention and found that the death was unlawfully caused in accordance with Section 189(b) of the Penal Code.

Section 196 (c) Uganda Penal Code: Where the victim dies in trying to escape

If the victim (V) brings about his own death under an apprehension, occasioned by the accused (A) of immediate violence to himself (V), the death can be attributed legally to the accused.' Card, Cross and Jones (1992:196)

CASE: In *Halliday* [1886-90] All ER 1028, the defendant had come home drunk and threatened his wife's life. She got half in and half out of a window and was held by her daughter. The defendant threatened the daughter who let the mother go and the mother fell to her death.

Held: The court held that if a man creates in another man's mind a sense of danger which causes such a person to try and escape, and in so doing that person is injured, the person who creates such a state of mind is responsible for the injuries which result.

CASE: *Uganda v Yoram Buchuruku & Others,* Criminal Case 201/91 (High Court) The accused persons were indicted for the murder of various victims under Section 183 of the Penal Code and one count of attempted murder under Section 197.

The prosecution case was that after the Amin regime problems arose in Kisiba village between the Muslims and others. On 26/06/79 during late morning to early evening, there was a rounding up of Muslims from the village. A large number of them were collected at a particular house, then herded to the river, surrounded by a large number of assailants. At the river a massacre occurred as the Muslims were attacked, cut and pushed into the River Rwizi. Some of the victims jumped into the river and while some swam and survived, some drowned and died.

Note: There were a number of different types of acts which resulted in the death of victims. In regard to the victims who jumped into the river, Justice D.C. Porter said in his judgement:

> Was the death of such victims caused by an unlawful act?

> The circumstance that caused victims to jump or fall into the water of their own volition to escape the violence actually happening at the riverside or occurring behind them is dealt with in Section 189(c) of the Penal Code, which can be paraphrased (to get rid of the superfluity of 'suches').

> A person is deemed to have caused the death of the deceased although his act is not the immediate or sole cause of death ... if by actual or threatened violence he causes the deceased to perform an act which causes his death, such act being a means of avoiding such violence which in the circumstances would appear natural to the deceased.

> Witness did jump into the river and survived: it would seem a natural thing to do in the circumstances if it was possible to get past the assailants to the river bank: if victims drowned doing so, the assailants would be responsible.

CASE: *R v Pitts* (1842) 174ER

The deceased threw himself into a river to avoid acts of intentional violence against him by the accused. The deceased drowned and the accused was held guilty of murder.

But according to Smith and Hogan, (1992:339) 'the test of causation to be applied is whether P's [the deceased] reaction was within the range of responses which might be expected from a victim in his situation.'

CASE: *Williams and Davis* [1992] Crim LR 198 cf *Roberts* (1971) 56 Crim App Rep 95 at 102:

> If the reaction was 'so daft as to make it [the victim's] own voluntary act' the chain of causation is broken. So it seems [the assaulter] does not have to take a 'daft' victim as he finds him – unless, presumably he knows him to be daft – i.e. likely to behave in an extraordinary fashion. The range of responses to be expected will of course vary according to the age and perhaps the sex of the victim.

CASE: *Republic v Msungwe* [1968] EA 203

The accused first assaulted the complainant and then chased him with a knife. Whilst running away from the accused, the complainant tried to jump over a furrow but fell and broke his leg. The accused left him lying semi-conscious. Eventually the complainant was taken to hospital and he had his leg amputated. The accused was convicted of doing grievous harm. On revision a question was raised: Whether the conviction could be supported when the injury to the complainant was not caused directly by the accused.

Held: the conviction was proper (*R v Halliday* applied)

Justice Biron said:

> ... the injury was caused by the complainant's attempting to jump over the furrow in fleeing from the accused. Even in the absence of any authority I would agree with the learned trial magistrate who said 'Although the accused did not hit in order to break the leg of the complainant, he technically did so by setting the motion of the whole system

which resulted into a grave injury on the complainant's leg. The complainant was at a big dilemma. If he stood within the reach of the accused he would no doubt be knifed. As he decided to run in escape, which is a natural thing, he fell into the ditch thereby losing his leg. Indeed, the accused attempted to do an act which would end, if not interfered with, in a felony. I would be inclined to agree with the learned magistrate and uphold the conviction, possibly if only by analogy with the definition of murder in the Penal Code, the relevant part which reads: 'A person is deemed to have caused the death of another person although his act is not the immediate or sole cause of death in any of the following cases: (c) if by actual or threatened violence he causes that other person to perform an act which causes the death of that person, such act being a means of avoiding such violence which in the circumstances would appear natural to the person whose death is so caused.'

Analogies, however close, and reasoning however strong, cannot by themselves create or even extend a criminal offence. There is however express authority to the point to wit R v Halliday (1889) where it was held: 'Where one person creates in the mind of another person such an immediate sense of danger as causes such other person to endeavour to escape, the person who created such a state of mind is responsible for any injuries which may result from his acts to the person endeavouring to escape.' The case is on all fours with this case before court.

Section 196 (d) Uganda Penal Code: Hastening the death of a dying person

The provision deals with cases in which a victim dies as a result of the cumulative effect of two or more unlawful injuries sustained in separate incidents.

Thus if A stabs V and shortly afterwards D stabs V, after which V dies from the cumulative effect of the two wounds, the second wound having aggravated the effect of the first, the death can be attributed to both A and D. This is legally possible although A and D did not act together and whether or not either wound was mortal in itself. (See Card, Cross and Jones, 1992:198). A would not, if charged with murder/manslaughter, successfully argue that his wound in itself was not mortal. D would also not successfully argue that it was only because the victim already had another wound that death occurred.

Smith and Hogan (1992:335) also assert that if D and E injure V in separate incidents, and the combination of their injuries lead to V's death, both D and E are guilty of homicide.

CASE: *R v Okute s/o Kaliebi* 8 EACA 78
Issue: The contribution of successive beatings to death.
The deceased was first beaten up by four men and made to dig up some stolen meat. Some time later, as the deceased, in a very weak condition, was being taken to the chief, he was assaulted by another man, X. The deceased died from shock resulting from the cumulative effect of his injuries. On appeal, it was held that the four men could not be held responsible for causing the deceased's death, as, on the evidence, it was possible that the injuries inflicted by them might not have caused death but for the subsequent assault by X. This distinguishes the case from *R v Enyaju s/o Oguruto* as there was no evidence of any common intention between the original beaters and X. But X was guilty of murder, for he had, with intent to cause grievous harm, assaulted one who was already in a very weak state.

Note: It was no defence for X to say that the injuries that he inflicted upon the deceased would not have caused death but for the prior assault. Generally an assailant must take his victim as he finds him.

CASE: *Uganda v L. Kakooza* Criminal Session Case No. 69/1991 (High Court)
The accused was indicted for the murder of his mother under Section 183 of the Penal Code. The accused grabbed his mother, threw her down, and kicked her. As a result she bled from her private parts and one intestine came out of her anus. She was taken to hospital but did not improve and died after a month. The cause of her death was a ruptured spleen and in the doctor's opinion, this was likely to have been caused by the assault.

Issue: (as stated by court) Whether the prosecution adduced sufficient evidence to prove that the kicks inflicted on the deceased caused the injury to the deceased's spleen, especially as death was not immediate.

Held:
1. Whether the spleen was already weak or the deceased was sickly is irrelevant. The accused would still be held responsible for the death under section 189(d). A person is deemed to have caused the death of another if by an act or omission he hastened the death of a person suffering under any disease or injury which ... from such act or omission would have caused death; even if, as suggested by the defence counsel, the injury to the spleen was due to a fall on a hard object it was the accused who threw her down. If that is how deceased sustained an injury to the spleen, the accused would still be responsible.
2. The accused had to take the deceased as he had found her. It is not a defence to say that the assault by the accused was not the sole cause of her death.

Section 196 (e) of the Uganda Penal Code: Contribution by third parties
It is no defence for an accused to plead that his/her act was not the sole cause of death. Although it can be proved that a third party's conduct also contributed to the death, an accused can be convicted of the death if his/her act was a substantial cause. As stated by Card, Cross and Jones (1992:195), it is not the function of the jury (read judge within Uganda's context) to evaluate competing causes or to choose which is dominant.

CASE: *R v Enyaju s/o Oguruto*, 12 EACA 42
During a tribal dance, T willfully gave the deceased a violent poke on the head with the sharper end of his heavy dancing stick, piercing the skull and causing the deceased's brain to protrude. The deceased fell to the ground, and almost immediately E beat him violently on the other side of the head, fracturing the skull. The trial judge specifically found that the deceased was still alive at the time of E's blow. Each injury would inevitably have caused the deceased's death.

Held: On appeal that both T and E were rightly convicted of the deceased's murder.

CASE: *Geoffrey Saaku v Uganda* Criminal Appeal No.4/1998 (Court of Appeal for Uganda)

The accused was indicted on two counts of murder contrary to Sections 183 and 184 of the Penal Code. According to the prosecution, on the relevant night, the appellant went to the house of deceased No.1 and called her to come out of the house to receive a gift from a third party.

Deceased No.1 came out of the house while carrying Deceased No.2 (a child of 2) on her back, and carrying a lamp in her hand. The caller (accused) gave Deceased No.1 a jerrycan containing fuel. As soon as D1 received the jerrycan from the accused, the jerrycan caught fire from the lamp. The two victims were burnt by the fire and died in hospital the following day.

The accused was convicted of murder.

The court of Appeal held that the trial judge was correct in holding the appellant guilty under Section 189(e) which provides:

> A person is deemed to have caused the death of another person although his act is not the immediate or sole cause of death … if his acts … would not have caused death unless it had been accompanied by an act or omission of the person killed …

Notes:

In relation to the present case, the accused carried an inflammable material in an open jerrycan. On the other hand he told the victim who was carrying fire to go close to him so that she could see her gift.

In other words, the accused's act (carrying an inflammable material in an open jerrycan) was accompanied by the act of the deceased (going close to the accused with fire). When the inflammable liquid came into contact with the fire from the lamp, it exploded into flames.

CASE: *Tindira s/o Chiru and Maria s/o Panduji v Rex* Criminal Appeals Nos. 88 and 89/1951 (East African Court of Appeal)

The two appellants were convicted of murder before the High Court of Tanganyika. Both accused, who were drunk and armed with sticks, intervened in a quarrel over a woman. The deceased, unarmed, came up and asked what was going on. The second appellant thereupon hit him a blow on the left temple with a bamboo stick from which the deceased's skull was cracked, and there was a haemorrhage. The first appellant then hit the deceased over the head with a heavy stick inflicting a wound skull-deep, fracturing his skull and there was bleeding from the brain. The cause of death was haemorrhage from this latter fracture.

The doctor's opinion was that a thin bamboo stick used with moderate force could have caused the cracking of the skull on the temple and the heavy stick or pole could have caused the wound on the crown of the head. He further gave his opinion that the effect of the fracture was necessarily fatal and that the crack over the temple if left untreated would also have proved fatal and that in conjunction with the fracture it accelerated death.

The court found no merit in the first appellant's appeal. In the appeal of the second appellant, two issues were considered:

1. Whether he can rightly be deemed to have caused the death of the deceased and if so,
2. Whether his offence was murder or manslaughter

Held: That although there was no evidence of common intention, the second appellant was rightly deemed to have caused death.

Judgement:

It is clear from the medical evidence that the injury he [the second appellant] inflicted on the deceased was not the immediate or sole cause of death, the immediate cause of which was the blow struck by the first appellant. We do not find evidence to support a common intention formed in the minds of the two appellants to attack the deceased. There is nothing to suggest that when either of the appellants struck his blow it was in pursuance of a preconceived plan. Nevertheless, we are of the opinion that the second appellant was rightly deemed to have caused death. The Penal Code of Tanganyika enacts:

A person is deemed to have caused the death of another person although his act is not the immediate or sole cause of death in any of the following case – (e) if his act or omission would not have caused death unless it had been accompanied by an act or omission of the person killed or of other persons.

… If the medical evidence were that the cracking of deceased's skull and consequent haemorrhage would not have caused death but for the deceased's own refusal to have medical attention or the omission of his relatives to obtain medical attention in good time, then under this paragraph, the appellant would be rightly deemed to have caused death. *A fortiori*, when the evidence is that the injury inflicted would of itself have caused death in due course. It matters not in such a case that death was accelerated by a later and more severe injury inflicted by another person.

CASE: *Uganda v Musene Swata* Criminal Session case No. 147/1972 (High Court) The accused was indicted for murder under Section 183 of the Penal Code.

The accused found the deceased stealing his cotton and arrested him and tied him up. The accused and others escorted the deceased towards the Gombolola Headquarters. On the way, the accused struck the deceased twice on the head with a stick. No satisfactory evidence was available as to what happened at the time the deceased met his death, which was soon afterwards. But those who answered the alarm found the accused and many people at the scene. There were two sticks other than the accused's stick and some stones beside the deceased's body. The cause of death was the fractures of the base of skull and spinal cord. The accused admitted striking the two blows on the back of the head but contended that the deceased's death had been caused by injuries inflicted by other villagers not charged.

Held *interalia* that it was difficult to pinpoint who had inflicted the fatal blow on the deceased. But the accused's assault contributed to and hastened the deceased's death within Section 189 of the Penal Code.

Editorial comment: The learned trial judge did not indicate what subsection he considered applicable but he appears to have acted under either subsection (d) or (e).

1. This however is not to say that the law does not protect the life of an unborn child. The extent to which the life of the unborn is protected will be dealt with under procuring of a miscarriage.)

2. See also Reeves (1839) 9C and p 25.

3. Cited in 'lecture notes htm Criminal Law Lecture Notes 1998/99 – Homicide: An Overview' – http: // privatewww.essex.ac.uk/- joash/homicide.htm. Accessed on 10/28/02.

4..See [1996] 1 Crim App Rep 351, [1996] Crim LR 268, which is the Court of Appeal judgement and the House of Lords judgement of 24 July 1997 at URL http://www.parliament

5. See e.g. Smith and Hogan 1992:330, Card, Cross and Jones, 1992:192)

6. Adopted from lecture notes...htm CRIMINAL LAW LECTURE NOTES 1998/99.Homicide: An Overview. http://privatewww.essex.ac.uk/~joash/homicide.htm. Accessed on 10/28/02

7. Any person who, being the parent, guardian or other person having the lawful care or charge of a child under the age of fourteen years, and being able to maintain such child, willfully and without lawful or reasonable cause deserts the child and leaves it without means of support, is guilty of a misdemeanour.

8. Any person who, being the parent or guardian or other person having the lawful care or charge of any child of tender years and unable to provide for itself, refuses or neglects (being able to do so) to provide sufficient food, clothes, bedding and other necessaries for such child, so as thereby to injure the health of such child, is guilty of a misdemeanour.

9. Section 2 Criminal Procedure Code Act already referred to)

10. Hennigan [1971]3 All ER 133; Cato [1976]1 All ER 260

11. see HENNIGAN [1971]3 All ER 133; GATO [1976]1 All ER 260, [1976]1 WLR 110, CA

12 Now 196(b)

13.Now 219

3

The Offence of Murder

The offence of murder is covered in Sections 188, 189, 191 of the Uganda Penal Code

Section 188

Any person who, *of malice aforethought*, causes the death of another person by an unlawful act or omission is guilty of murder. [My emphasis]

Section 189

Any person convicted of murder shall be sentenced to death.

Section 191

Malice aforethought shall be deemed to be established by evidence providing either of the following circumstances:

a) An intention to cause the death of any person, whether such person is the person actually killed or not.

b) Knowledge that the act or omission causing death will probably cause the death of some person, whether such person is the person actually killed or not, although such knowledge is accompanied by indifference whether death is caused or not, or by a wish that it may not be caused.

Murder is a crime of specific intent

Malice aforethought is the mental element for murder. It can either be expressed by the party or implied by law. Intention in the context of murder includes direct as well as indirect intent.

Direct intent covers the situation where the defendant desires the death as represented in Section 191 (a).

Indirect intent covers the situation where the death is foreseen by the accused as virtually certain, although not desired for its own sake. Indirect intent is catered for under Section 191(b).

The distinction between murder and manslaughter (involuntary manslaughter) rests upon the presence of malice aforethought in murder, and its absence in manslaughter. As Clarkson and Keating [1998:633] note 'Defining the parameters of murder is *primarily* a task of defining malice aforethought, the *mens rea* of murder.[1]

In a murder case therefore, the prosecution must prove beyond reasonable doubt each and every ingredient mentioned below – which include those common to all homicides:

1. That the victim was a human being.
2. The fact of death.
3. That death occurred within a year and a day.

4. The cause of death.
5. That the killing was unlawful.
6. That it was the accused who was responsible.
7. That the killing was done with malice aforethought.

CASE: In *Uganda v Kadidi alias Kabagambe* [1992-1993]
The High Court of Uganda held interalia that in a case of murder, the prosecution must prove beyond reasonable doubt that the deceased is dead and that the killing was unlawful and that it was the accused who killed the deceased and that in killing him, he had malice aforethought. The accused must also prove that the accused has no defence available to him.

See also *Kassim Obura and Another v Uganda* [1981] HCB 9.

CASE: In *Uganda v Peter Ogwang* Criminal Session Case No.306/1992
The High Court cited *Mancini v DPP* [1942] AC 1; *Didasi Kabengi v Uganda* [1970] EA 405 (Court of Appeal for Uganda); *Eria Galikuwa v R* [1951] 18 EACA 175 and stated that it is the duty of the trial court to deal with all the alternative defences, if any, if they emerge from all the evidence as fit for consideration notwithstanding that they are not put forward or raised by the defence, for every man on trial for murder is entitled to have the issue of manslaughter left for the assessors if there is evidence on which such a verdict can be given him. To deprive him of this, constitutes a grave miscarriage of justice.

CASE: *Mancini v DPP* [1942] AC 1 (House of Lords)
Held *inter alia* that: On the trial of a person with murder it is the duty of the judge in his summing-up to deal adequately with any view of evidence which might reduce the crime to manslaughter. The fact that the defending counsel may not have stressed the possibility of such an alternative case does not relieve the judge from directing the jury to consider it, if there is material which justifies such a direction, but the possibility of manslaughter instead of murder arises only when the evidence is such as might satisfy the jury as the judges of fact that the elements are present which would so reduce the crime, or might induce a reasonable doubt whether this may not be the right view.

Judgement: The court stated that:

> To avoid all possible misunderstanding, ... this is far from saying that in every trial for murder, where the accused pleads not guilty, the judge must include in his summing up to the jury, on the subject of manslaughter. The possibility of a verdict of manslaughter instead of murder only arises when the evidence given is such as might satisfy that the elements were present which would reduce the crime to manslaughter, or, at any rate, might induce a reasonable doubt whether this was, or was not the case.

Plea of guilty on a murder charge
CASE: *Tomasi Mufumu* [1959] EA 625
The appellant had speared to death one L. who had earlier on the same day killed the appellant's son. When arraigned for murder, the appellant said 'I speared him to death as he killed my son the same day.' His advocate informed the court that he had advised

the appellant to plead guilty as in his opinion he had no possible defence to the charge. The trial judge then heard counsel for the prosecution and thereafter convicted the appellant of murder and sentenced him to death. The appellant appealed on the ground that he did not know that the sentence for murder was death.

Held: It was clear that the appellant's plea was not an unequivocal plea of guilty of murder and might as well have been a plea of killing upon provocation and this vitiated the conviction.

Per curium: '… it is very desirable that a trial judge, on being offered a plea which he construes as a plea of guilty in a murder case, should not only satisfy himself that the plea is an unequivocal plea, but should satisfy himself also and record that the accused understands the elements which constitute the offence of murder … and understands that the penalty is death.'

Malice aforethought

As L.B. Curzon [1997:131] said: 'Malice aforethought' is a term of art when used in the context of the crime of murder, and its meaning cannot be determined by reference to the everyday use of the words 'malice' and 'aforethought'. As put by Card, Cross and Jones [1992] *Criminal Law* page 201:

> Malice aforethought does not imply either premeditation or ill-will. The sudden intentional killing of one's nearest and dearest is no less murder than the cunningly contrived assassination of a deadly enemy.

Smith and Hogan [1992:346] said of the phrase malice aforethought:

> The phrase it has been truly said 'is a mere arbitrary symbol …, for the "malice" may have in it nothing really malicious; and need never be really "aforethought"'. Thus a parent who kills a suffering child out of motives of compassion is 'malicious' for this purpose.

What is relevant is that the parent's conduct, which led to the death, was performed with the aim that death occurs. It is the fact that the accused aimed at the death of a person as the consequence of her/his conduct that makes her/him criminally liable, and not the motive which accompanied the conduct. Thus, a person (A) who kills another, out of compassion in order to save the 'victim' from suffering (e.g. from long illness) is as guilty of murder as one (B) who kills in order to inherit the property of the deceased. Although A's motive may be noble it does not give legitimacy to his intention.

Furthermore there is sufficient aforethought if an intention to kill is formed only a second before the fatal blow is struck. Thus in *Uganda v Waiswa* [1977] 300 Justice Ssekandi held *inter alia* that:

> An intention to kill may be formed at the moment of assault; an accused need not have the intention to kill prior to the assault.

For malice aforethought to exist therefore, neither ill-will nor premeditation is necessary

Actus reus and *mens rea*: In murder, the consequence of the unlawful conduct must be the death of a human being. Death of a human being is thus part of the *actus reus* of murder and indeed of other homicides. Furthermore, that *actus reus* must have been accompanied by a specific intention, i.e. the intention to cause the death of a human being, before one is guilty of murder. Consequently, if the intention of an accused (A) was to kill a dog, but he unfortunately ends up killing a human being, such person would not be guilty of murder. And where A intends to kill a person but misses and kills a dog, he cannot be guilty of murder since the consequence which the law is interested in punishing under murder is the death of a human being.

CASE: In the Tanzanian case of *Sultan Maginga* [1969] HCB 33.
The deceased and a woman were lying in a rice field after sexual intercourse. Sultan Maginga, who had gone to guard his rice fields against wild pigs, saw movement of grass and called out if there was anybody. There was no reply. Thinking it was a pig, he threw a spear and it landed on the deceased and killed him.

It was held that the charge of murder could not be sustained because it was a clear case of mistake of fact. The accused had no *mens rea*.

Intention to kill a human being: Transferred malice

It is however important to note that where A intends to kill a specific person (B), but instead kills (V), A will still be guilty of murder. As indicated in Section 191, what is important is that the accused intended to kill a human being and in fact killed a human being. The fact that the intended victim 'escaped' does not affect the actor's criminal liability.

CASE: In *Paulo s/o Mabula v R* [1953] 20 EACA 207
The appellant killed his wife. It was common ground that the deceased died as a result of a knife wound in her chest which she received while endeavouring to prevent the appellant from cutting his throat. The appellant contended that the injury was accidental, although it was argued by the prosecution that the appellant had intentionally injured the victim. *(See also* under Chapter 1, Unlawful acts)

Held *inter alia* by the East African Court of appeal that:

> Where as a result of an act by an accused intended to kill himself, another is killed, he is properly convicted of murder, even if he did not intend to kill that other person.

In the Court's judgement, it was pointed out that *malice aforethought constitutes an intention to cause the death of any person, whether such person is the person actually killed or not.*

In this case, the courts applied what scholars refer to as the *principle of transferred malice*. Smith and Hogan (1992:74) explain:

> If D, with the *mens rea* of a particular crime, does an act which causes the *actus reus* of the same crime, he is guilty, even though the result, in some respects, is an unintended one. D intends to murder O and, in the dusk, shoots at a man whom he believes to be O. He hits and kills the man at whom he aims, who is in fact P. In one sense this is obviously an unintended result; but D did intend to cause the *actus reus* which he has caused and is guilty of murder.

Smith and Hogan further explain:

> The law, however, carries this principle still further. Suppose, now, that D, intending to murder O, shoots at a man who is in fact O, but misses and kills P who, unknown to D, was standing close by. This is an unintended result in a different – and more fundamental – respect than the example considered above. Yet once again, D, with the *mens rea* of a particular crime, has caused the *actus reus* of the same crime; and once again, he is guilty of murder.

We however have to remember that in criminal law, the *mens rea* and *actus reus* must coincide and this puts a limit to the applicability of the principle of transferred malice. Smith and Hogan (1992:75) thus note:

> It is important to notice the limitations of this doctrine. *It operates only when the actus reus and the mens rea of the same crime coincide.* If D, with the *mens rea* of one crime, does an act which causes the *actus reus* of a different crime, he cannot, as a general rule, be convicted of either offence. D shoots at P's dog with intention to kill it but misses and kills P who, unknown to D, was standing close by. Obviously he cannot be criminally liable for killing the dog, for he has not done so; nor can he be convicted of murder, for he has not the *mens rea* for that crime.[2] A similar result follows where D shoots at P with intent to kill him and, quite accidentally, kills P's dog: D is guilty of neither crime.[3] [Emphasis mine]

Section 191 (b): Knowledge that the unlawful conduct will probably cause death.

CASE: *Sentongo v Uganda* [1975] HCB 240 EACA [Law, Ag. P., Mustafa, Ag. V-P & Musoke, J.A)

The appellants were jointly charged and convicted of murder contrary to Section 183 of the Uganda Penal Code.

At the time of the commission of the offence the appellants were employed as askaris at a Gombolola Headquarters. The deceased stole a bunch of bananas from his master. After his arrest he was escorted to the Gombolola Headquarters by six or seven men. On arrival at the Headquarters both appellants questioned the deceased who admitted his guilt. Thereupon, the appellants went to a store and came back with sticks. They made the deceased lie down and beat him severely with the sticks. They finally flung him into a cell where he was found dead the next morning. At the trial the sticks were not produced in evidence. However, they were described by witnesses as 'long' and 'slightly big'.

The learned trial judge found malice aforethought clearly established both from the actions of the appellants in wantonly and continually assaulting the deceased with sticks and in the nature of the injuries and their extent.

On appeal held:

1. Under Section 186 of the Penal Code malice aforethought is established by evidence showing an intention to cause death or knowledge that the act or omission will probably cause death. In this case, there was neither motive nor intention on the part of the appellants to kill the deceased.

2. It was not within the knowledge of the appellants that the beating of the deceased with sticks was likely to cause death as the sticks were kept available in the store for the purpose of beating and not killing.
3. The deceased died as a result of the unlawful beating administered by the appellants. Accordingly, the appellants were guilty of manslaughter.

Conclusion:: Since the description of the sticks did not indicate that they were very dangerous, the court came to the conclusion that the accused persons could not be said to have had knowledge that the unlawful conduct (the beating) would probably cause death.

CASE: *Mugao & Another v R* [1972] EA 543
The two appellants and others beat up Muruki (the deceased) and M'Ngirani who were suspected of having stolen a goat and eating it. The suspects were beaten with long, thin, green branches to obtain information as to the whereabouts of the remains of the goat. Muruki was then placed in a hut for the night, guarded by the owner of the goat, an old man. M'Ngirani was released. By the next day Muruki had died.

Three days later a post mortem failed to reveal any external injuries due to advanced decomposition of the body. The doctor conducting the post mortem expressed his opinion that the deceased's death was due to cerebral concussion following a head injury caused by a blunt weapon such as a stick or by a heavy fall.

In the High Court all seven men including the two appellants were tried for murder. All accused were acquitted save the two appellants who had confessed that they had beaten the deceased. They were convicted of murder.

Held *inter alia*:
In view of the weapon chosen, no intention to cause death had been proved.

Judgement read by Law, Ag. V R. The issue was whether malice aforethought had been proved:

> ... clearly there was no evidence establishing an intention to kill within para (a) of s 206 to wit an intention to cause the death ... (Kenyan equivalent of Section 186(a) Uganda Penal Code)

> ... Had the appellants intended to kill or do grievous harm they would not have selected light sticks with which to beat the deceased. We have no doubt on the evidence that the intention ... by inflicting pain, was to obtain information as to the whereabouts of a stolen goat.

> s.206 (b) knowledge that the act or omission will probably cause the death ... although such knowledge is accompanied by indifference whether death ... is caused or not

> The state submitted that the evidence established malice aforethought within Para (b) of s. 206. That as reasonable men, the appellants must have anticipated that their prolonged assault on the 2 suspects, although it was not intended to cause death or grievous bodily harm at the time, was likely eventually to cause grievous bodily harm and death [the state relied on D.P.P. v Smith [1960]3 All ER 161] ...

The court said:

The position, as we see it, is that the appellants and others joined together in beating 2 suspects with light sticks ... They had no intention to kill or do grievous harm. They desisted from the beating, after it had lasted a long time, and released one suspect. The fact that this man was not detained in hospital is some indication of the nature of the beating administered by the appellants. The deceased was placed in a hut under the guard of 2 other persons. There is no evidence that the deceased received the blow which caused his death, for which a heavy blunt instrument must have been used, whilst being beaten by the appellants. The possibility cannot be excluded that the blow was struck when the deceased was in the custody of the guards . . . The appellants could not in our view have reasonably anticipated such a thing happening in their absence nor is there any evidence that they had a common intention with the guards that further violence should be done to the deceased after their departure. We do not think that the death was, on the evidence, a probable consequence of the prosecution of the common unlawful purpose of beating the deceased with light sticks, so as to involve the appellants in criminal responsibility for his subsequent death. The reasonable possibility of death having been caused by he independent, unforeseen and not reasonably anticipated act of a third cannot be excluded.

Result: Conviction quashed.

CASE: *Hyam v DPP* [1974] 2 All ER 41

The appellant (Hyam) drove to the house where Mrs B was living with her son and two daughters, and set B's house on fire. As a result of the fire, Mrs B's two daughters were killed. The appellant was charged with their murder. She admitted that she realised that what she had done was very dangerous to anyone living in the house but said she did not intend to cause death. She was jealous of Mrs B, whom she believed to be about to marry J (J was the appellant's lover), and her motive in starting the fire was to frighten Mrs B into leaving the neighbourhood.

The House of Lords held that to establish the *mens rea* of murder, it was sufficient to prove that, when the accused performed the relevant acts, he knew that it was probable that those acts would result in grievous harm to somebody, even though he did not desire to bring that result about. Lord Diplock stated thus:

> In murder no distinction is to be drawn between the state of mind of one who does an act because he desires to produce a particular evil consequence (death) and the state of mind of one who does an act knowing that it is likely to produce that consequence, although it may not be the object he was seeking to achieve by doing the act.

CASE: *Uganda v L. Kakooza* Criminal Session Case No. 69 of 1991 (High Court)

The accused was indicted for the murder of his mother under Section 183. The accused grabbed his mother, threw her down, and kicked her. As a result she bled from her private parts and one intestine came out of her anus. She was taken to hospital but did not improve and died after a month. The cause of her death was a ruptured spleen and in the doctor's opinion, this was likely caused by assault. (See also below.)

Issues: The trial judge framed one of the issues as follows:

> Has the prosecution proved beyond reasonable doubt that the accused deliberately

kicked his mother on a vulnerable part of her abdomen to cause her death or that in doing so he ought to have known that it could probably result in her death?

Held *inter alia*:

> I am unable to say with certainty that the accused deliberately kicked his mother in the manner in which he did with the specific intention of killing her. Neither is there conclusive evidence to show that the accused knew or ought to have known that the probable result of such an assault would be death.

> It is now settled that a court of law is not bound in law to infer malice aforethought by reason only of the result of an accused's actions being a natural or probable consequence of those actions. The court should decide whether the accused did intend or foresee that result by reference to all the evidence drawing such inference from the evidence as appear proper in the circumstances. See *U v George William Otim* 1977 HCB 286; *U v Wilbert Sekandi & Another* 1972 HCB 109; *U v Leo Masaba & Waibi* 1971 HCB 275.

Murder a crime of specific intent: Intention to cause grievous harm does not constitute malice aforethought[4]

CASE: *Bukenya & Others v Uganda* [1972] EA549. (East African Court of Appeal) The appellants were convicted of murder after having beaten the deceased with sticks and a stone. The trial judge found that their intention was to cause death or grievous bodily harm.

On appeal **held**: Malice aforethought is not constituted by an intention to cause grievous bodily harm.

Judgement read by Lutta:

> ... it is clear that an intention to cause grievous bodily harm no longer constitutes an element in establishing malice aforethought.[5]   The Chief Justice has found that the intention of the appellants was to cause death or grievous bodily harm. In view of his findings, the offence committed could either be murder or manslaughter. Since there is doubt as to which offence was committed, the doubt must be resolved in favour of the appellants.

Result: Conviction for murder set aside. Manslaughter substituted.

CASE: *Rujumba v Uganda* [1992-1993] HCB36 (Supreme Court) The appellant was convicted of murder and sentenced to death. The salient facts were that the appellant, a youth of between 18 and 20 years of age, used a stick in jabbing or poking his mother on the upper part of the abdomen. There was one assault only. The trial judge found that the stick used to cause death was a blunt object of smooth surface and that such was the object that led to the blow which caused the injuries that led to the deceased's death. It was not known how heavy the stick used actually was and the trial judge came to the finding that the intent was to cause grievous harm.

Held:

1. An intent to cause harm *no longer* constitutes an element in establishing malice aforethought. The evidence on record in the instant case, was not such as to warrant the

inference of the intention to murder or of knowledge that the blow could probably cause death. It was an unusual result from such a blow and that being the case there was not the requisite *mens rea* for murder within the wording of Section 186 of the Penal Code. [My emphasis]

2. There should always be evidence that the alleged weapon that was used to cause death was described to the Doctor or was actually observed by the Doctor who performed the post mortem examination, and in whose opinion, the weapon was consistent with the nature and type of the assault and its effect on the deceased, if that is the truth. It was not simply that the injuries were caused by a blunt object, but that the blunt object in the case could have been used to cause the injuries, in the way it was alleged to have been used. This was important in estimating the *mens rea* of an accused.

Murder a crime of specific intent: Any doubt as to the existence of intention to kill is to the benefit of the accused

CASE: *Uganda v L. Kakooza*, Criminal Session Case No. 69/1991 (High Court, before Justice Mukasa-Kikonyogo)

The accused was often heard threatening the deceased (his mother) with death. On the night of 3/07/89 the accused grabbed the deceased and threw her out of her house. He kicked her and beat her. An alarm was raised which was answered by PW5 and others. According to PW5, he found the accused kneeling on the deceased, holding her neck with one hand whilst the other was holding a panga against her neck. PW5 and others got hold of the accused and overpowered him. Thereafter, the accused said that although he had been stopped from killing the deceased, he would kill her anyway. The accused was handed over to the authorities. Meanwhile the deceased was bleeding from her private parts and one intestine had come out of her anus. She was taken to hospital and admitted. Realizing that she was going to die, the deceased requested that she be discharged so that she could die at home. She died three days after her discharge. The cause of her death was raptured spleen, most likely caused by assault. The accused was charged with murder under Section 183 of the Penal Code.

Issue: Whether the accused had malice aforethought, and specific intent.

Held *inter alia:*

Has the prosecution proved beyond reasonable doubt that the accused deliberately kicked his mother on a vulnerable part of her abdomen to cause her death or that in doing so he ought to have known that it could probably result in her death? ... I agree that the accused's conduct before, during and after the assault coupled with prior threats of death raises grave suspicion that he had intended to kill his mother. Perhaps had it not been for the intervention by her grandchildren the accused would have probably cut her throat with a panga. Strong as this suspicion may be it is not in itself proof of specific intention on the part of the accused to kill. It could even be argued for him that wild as he was by uttering threats of death and placing a panga against the deceased's neck he had only intended to scare her out of her wits so that she vacated her land for him to sell. It would also be asked why did he not cut her immediately on arrival or just after pulling her out of the house or why had he not done so by the time PW5 answered the alarm?

I concede that, that sort of conduct and actions are hard to defend but there is some room for doubt since the accused did not cause the death of the deceased by cutting her with a panga.

Turning to the kicking which caused the injury to the spleen which eventually resulted in the deceased's death … I am unable to say with certainty that the accused deliberately kicked his mother in the manner in which he did with the specific intention of killing her . Neither is there conclusive evidence to show that the accused knew or ought to have known that the probable result of such an assault would be death.

It is now settled that a court of law is not bound in law to infer malice aforethought by reason only of the result of an accused's actions being a natural or probable consequence of those actions. The court should decide whether the accused did intend or foresee that result by reference to all the evidence drawing such inference from the evidence as appear proper in the circumstances. [see *U v George William Otim* 1977 HCB 286; *U v Wilbert Sekandi and Anor* 1972 HCB 109, *U v Leo Masaba and Waibi* 1971 HCB 275]

… even where there are no defences available to an accused charged with murder, like in the present case, it would still be open to the court to conclude that although the accused acted unjustifiably he had no intention to kill or cause serious bodily injury then manslaughter should be the verdict. … In the case before court … the prosecution has not proved malice aforethought on the part of the accused beyond reasonable doubt. There is room for some doubt which would be resolved in favour of the accused.

Murder and intoxication

The possible effect of intoxication on an accused's responsibility on a murder charge is provided for in Section 12 of the Penal Code Act. Although intoxication is a general 'defence' and not specific to murder, it is often relevant in regard to the issue of malice aforethought.

CASE: In *Uganda v Sempija Samuel* Criminal Case No. 243/98, the High Court gave a useful exposition on the effect of intoxication on criminal responsibility thus:

In general, intoxication is not a defence to a criminal charge (S. 13 (1) P.C.) But there may be a defence where intoxication is involuntary (S 13 (2) (a) P.C.) and even voluntary intoxication may have some mitigating effect on criminal liability.

Under Section 12 (4) it is provided that:

Intoxication shall be taken into account for the purpose of determining whether the person charged had formed any intention, specific or otherwise, in the absence of which he or she would not be guilty of the offence.

As the cases below will indicate courts make a distinction between cases of insanity produced by drunkenness and of drunkenness falling short of insanity but negativing intent.

CASE: *Antonio Lwasa v Uganda* Criminal Appeal No. 29/95. Supreme Court of Uganda The Supreme Court cited the Court of Appeal for Eastern Africa in *R v Kingori s/o Kibiro* (1932) 14 KLR 135, where it was observed:

Whether intoxication establishes absence of *mens rea* or not, is a question of fact. The penal code lays down not that a person being intoxicated is evidence that he is incapable of forming an intention, but that if the court is satisfied that by reason of intoxication a person is incapable of forming an intention then he will be excused not by reason of such intoxication, but by reason of the absence of intention.

Thus an accused need not specifically raise the defence, what is important is whether on the facts before court, there is reason to believe, on a balance of probabilities, that the accused was not capable of forming the required specific intent.

See also *Tukwasiibwe James v Uganda* Criminal Appeal 6/1996. Court of Appeal

The effect of intoxication: Murder needs specific intent

CASE: *Nyakite s/o Oyugi v R* [1959] EA 322 (East African Court of Appeal)
The appellant was convicted of murder on the evidence of five eyewitnesses. The evidence of the prosecution and that of the appellant himself established that the appellant had been drinking, but at the trial neither the appellant nor his advocate raised the issue of intoxication as affecting his liability, the defence being that the appellant did not kill the deceased. Since there was ample evidence to support the conviction the only point which the court found it necessary to consider was a misdirection by the trial judge regarding the burden of proving whether the appellant in spite or because of intoxication, was or was not capable of forming the specific intention necessary to establish a charge of murder.

Held: The trial judge erred in directing himself that the burden of raising a defence of intoxication so as to negative an intent to kill was on the accused.

Judgement read by Justice Windham:

> The true position in law is embodied in *Director of Public Prosecutions Vs Beard* [1920] A.C 479 regarding the relevance of evidence of an accused's intoxication in a murder charge, and in *Woolmington V DPP* [1935] A.C 462 and *Mancini v DPP* [1942] A.C regarding the burden of proof generally in criminal cases...

> It is of course correct that if the accused seeks to set up a defence of insanity by reason of intoxication, the burden of establishing that defence rests upon him in that he must at least demonstrate the probability of what he seeks to prove. *But if the plea is merely that the accused was by reason of intoxication incapable of forming the specific intention required to constitute murder . . . the onus is not on the accused.* [My emphasis][6]

CASE: See also *Uganda v Lazaro Daniel Idubale* Criminal Session Case 84/95 wherein the High Court of Uganda held that where there is evidence that an accused had consumed a considerable amount of alcohol, it would be unsafe to convict such accused of murder because there is a probability that such accused person would not be capable of forming the specific intent to kill. In such circumstances a verdict of guilty of manslaughter would be returned.

Once there is evidence of the probability that an accused was drunk at the time of commission of an offence, the prosecution has the duty to prove that the accused was not so drunk as to be incapable of forming an intent to kill.

Burden of proof for intoxication

CASE: *Malungu s/o Kieti v R* [1959] EA797 (East African Court of Appeal)
The appellant was convicted of murder. The evidence established that the appellant

was drunk at the time he killed the deceased. The assessors were of the opinion that the appellant was incapable of forming the intent necessary to constitute the offence of murder but the trial judge took the view that the onus of rebutting the presumption that he was capable of forming the necessary intention to kill was on the appellant.

On appeal **held:**
1. The burden of proving that an accused is capable of forming the intent necessary to constitute the offence of murder always remains on the prosecution.
2. Since it was not certain whether the judge on a proper direction would have necessarily reached the same conclusion the conviction of murder could not stand.

Result: Appeal allowed. Conviction of murder set aside and manslaughter substituted.

CASE: *Antonio Lwasa v Uganda* Criminal Appeal No. 9/95. Supreme Court of Uganda
The Supreme Court cited the Court of Appeal for Eastern Africa in *Cheminingwa v R* (1956) 23 EACA 451 and *Kongoro s/o Mrisho v R* (1956) 23 EACA 532 where it was held that:

> While the burden of proving insanity as a result of intoxication is on the accused, the burden is not on the accused to prove that due to intoxication he was incapable of forming the specific intent required for an offence e.g. to kill ... necessary to prove malice aforethought in a case of murder, the burden of proof being on the prosecution throughout.

CASE: *Ilanda s/o Kisongo v R* [1960] EA 780
The appellant had been convicted of the murder of his concubine. The evidence showed that when last seen with the deceased he was very drunk and that the deceased was killed by one blow on the chest with a stick. In summing up the case for the assessors, the judge gave no detailed direction that once evidence indicating that the mind of the appellant might have been affected by drink, it was for the prosecution to prove beyond reasonable doubt that the appellant was still capable of forming the necessary intent.

Held *inter alia* that the direction given on the question of intent ought to have been coupled with an explicit direction that it was not for the appellant to prove that he was so drunk as to be incapable of forming an intent to kill ... but that it was for the prosecution to prove beyond reasonable doubt that the appellant was not so affected as to disable him from forming the necessary intent.

CASE: *Rafairi Muzoora v Uganda* Criminal Appeal No. 15/1983, Supreme Court
Held that on a charge of murder, if the facts reveal the presence of alcohol in the accused at the time of the offence, even if the accused does not raise the question of intoxication as having affected his liability, the prosecution has the burden of showing that the appellant was capable of forming the specific intent to kill. Prosecution has the burden to prove that the accused was not so intoxicated as to be incapable of forming the requisite intent.

Where it is proved on a balance of probabilities, that the accused was affected by intoxication and was therefore incapable of forming the specific intent to kill, a verdict of manslaughter will be returned.

Proof of malice aforethought

Earlier cases cited dealing with malice aforethought emphasise the need to prove the presence of malice aforethought. The cases here discuss what guides the court in establishing whether malice was present.

Malice aforethought not presumed

CASE: *Lokoya v Uganda* [1968] EA 332

The appellant was convicted of murder. The killing occurred at night and the evidence was confused, but it appeared that the deceased had died from spear wounds inflicted on him by the appellant after an alarm had been raised. Although it was found as a fact that the appellant inflicted injuries on the deceased, the prosecution adduced no evidence as to what exactly happened before and at the moment of killing.

Issue: Whether the appellant acted with malice aforethought.

Held: The burden was on the prosecution to prove malice aforethought and that burden had not been discharged.

As that burden had not been discharged the conviction of murder could not stand. However, since the court was in no doubt that it was the appellant who killed the deceased, and that the killing was unlawful, a conviction of manslaughter was substituted.

Malice aforethought a state of mind

CASE: *Uganda v Natseba, Mushikoma Watete & Others* Criminal Session Case No. 283/97

Because malice aforethought is a state of mind or mental disposition it is not capable of being proved by direct evidence. It is deduced or gathered from the circumstances that accompany the commission of the offence in question.

Malice aforethought not capable of positive proof but can be implied from the accused's overt acts

CASE: *Uganda v Sempija Samuel* Criminal Case No. 243/98 (High Court of Uganda)
In his judgement, Justice Katutsi said *inter alia* that:

> Prosecution must prove malice aforethought. It has been said elsewhere that 'intention is not capable of positive proof; it can only be implied from overt facts. Setrena [1951] 13 WACA' I would respectively agree. Prosecution has presented evidence to show that the accused speared the deceased and then proudly stated ' have finished him'. ... later he went back to the deceased and (finding him still alive) uttered the words: 'You are not yet dead?'

> ... In the instant case the deceased was assaulted with a panga which is considered a dangerous or deadly weapon see *Uganda vs Turomwe* [1978] HCB and Section 273 (2) of the Penal Code Act. Wounds from which she died were inflicted on her head apart which is considered to be very vulnerable. ... the prosecution has established beyond reasonable doubt that the unlawful death was caused with malice aforethought.

See under *Malice aforethought and the use of weapons* for rulings that malice aforethought can be inferred from the use of a dangerous weapon on a vulnerable part of the body.

Conclusion: Malice aforethought can be inferred from:
1. The conduct of the accused before and after the assault
2. The nature of the weapon used
3. The part of the body aimed at

Conduct of the accused
Malice aforethought can be inferred from the conduct of the accused immediately before or after the assault
CASE: *Uganda v Sebastiano Otti* [1994-95] HCB 21
Held *inter alia*:

> In deciding whether malice aforethought has been established or not the court must look at the surrounding circumstances of the particular case, that is, the conduct of the accused immediately before or immediately after the incident, the nature of injury inflicted and the weapon used

CASE: *Geofrey Saaku v Uganda* Criminal Appeal No. 4/ 1998. Court of Appeal (see p.35 for case details.)
Malice aforethought was deduced from the following factors:
1. The previous threat by the accused to harm the deceased.
2. The accused called the deceased to come outside her house at night under false pretence.
3. The accused handed the deceased inflammable material which is a dangerous commodity.
4. The accused's conduct in running away after handing the deceased an open jerrycan which was likely to come into contact with the lamp she was holding.

Conclusion: The conduct of an accused before, at, and after the unlawful act can be a manifestation of malice aforethought.

CASE: In *Uganda v Lazaro Daniel Idubale* (Criminal Session Case No. 84/95) (High Court)
The conduct of the accused immediately after the assault was used to infer the presence of malice aforethought.

Previous threats as evidence of malice aforethought
CASE: In *Kifamunte Henry v Uganda* Criminal Appeal No. 10/1997
The Supreme Court held *inter alia* that in an indictment for murder, evidence of previous threats is relevant. Such evidence shows an expression of intention. It goes beyond mere motive and tends to connect the accused person with killing.
Cited with approval *Waibi and Another* [1968] EA 228; *Okecha s/o Olilia v R* (1940) Vol 7 EACA 74)

Malice aforethought and the use of weapons

In determining the issue of malice aforethought factors such as those enumerated below are taken into consideration.

1. The weapon used.
2. The manner in which it is used.
3. The part of the body injured.

The case of Tubere was cited with approval by the Supreme Court in *George Kanalusasi v Uganda*, Criminal Appeal 10/88.

It was stated that in determining the issue of malice aforethought, regard must be had to the nature of the weapon used, how the weapon was used and the part of the body aimed at.

Malice aforethought can be proved from circumstantial evidence: Use of a gun shows malice aforethought

CASE: *Uganda v Okello* [1992-1993] HCB 68 (High Court)
Held *inter alia* that:

> to prove murder, it must be shown that: the deceased is dead, his death was unlawfully caused, it was caused by the accused, with malice aforethought. ... The burden is on the prosecution ... to prove the case beyond reasonable doubt. "Beyond reasonable doubt" means that the evidence adduced must carry a reasonable degree of probability of the accused's guilt leaving only a very remote possibility in his favour.'

> Okello held further that 'malice aforethought is a mental element, but it is now established that it can be proved from surrounding circumstances e.g. weapon used, part of the body and nature of the injuries. The use of a gun shows malice aforethought.'

Malice aforethought: part of body assaulted, nature of weapon used

CASE: *Peter Wetusa and 2 Others v Uganda* Criminal Appeal No. 50/1998 (Supreme Court)

The court held *inter alia* that malice aforethought can be inferred from the nature of the weapon used (in this particular case a loaded gun) and the part of the deceased's body shot at (the chest).

Conclusion:
1. The chest is a vulnerable part of the body
2. A loaded gun is a lethal weapon.

See also *Kwesiga John alias Tumwesige v Uganda*, Criminal Appeal No.12/1999. (Court of Appeal for Uganda.) where the Court of Appeal for Uganda agreed with the High Court ruling that malice aforethought could be inferred from the use of a lethal weapon on vulnerable parts of the body.

CASE: *Uganda v Ssebuguzi & Others* [1988-1990] HCB 18. (High Court)
Held *inter alia*: Malice aforethought can be found in the nature of weapons used and what part of the body such weapon was applied. The deceased was hit with a hoe twice on the head. The doctors' evidence clearly showed that the deceased's head was cracked on two areas and there was internal bleeding. It was clear from the

above evidence that the person who killed the deceased, hitting him on the head with a hoe, desired the death of the deceased or knew that the deceased would die from such injuries. He therefore killed with malice aforethought.

See also *Uganda v Yusuf Wamalwa Walimbwa* Criminal Session Case No. 51/1993. (High Court) where justice Engwau also restated the law that the nature of weapon used and the part of the body aimed at are factors to be taken into consideration in determining the presence of malice aforethought. The gun was said to be a deadly weapon and the chest a vulnerable part of the body.

The Supreme Court of Uganda has restated most of the principles mentioned above in as far as proof of malice aforethought is concerned. In *George Kanalusasi v Uganda*, the court cited *R v Tubere* with approval and stated that in a case of murder, it is incumbent on the trial judge to direct the assessors in terms of section 186 of the penal code which defines malice aforethought. It is incumbent on the trial judge to direct the assessors that regard must be had to the nature of weapon used, how that weapon was used and the part of the body injured in order to determine whether there was malice aforethought or not.

Malice aforethought deduced from manner in which a weapon is used

CASE: In *Rex v Tubere s/o Ochen* Criminal Appeal No. 84/1945 (Court of Appeal for Eastern Africa) (Appeal from decision of H.M. H/C of Uganda) the appellant appealed from a conviction of murder. It was proved that he had seriously assaulted the deceased with a heavy walking stick, causing severe injuries from which the deceased died shortly afterwards.

Held *inter alia*:
1. In arriving at a conclusion as to whether malice aforethought has been established the court must consider, the weapon used, the manner in which it is used and the part of the body injured.
3. Although an inference of malice will flow more readily from the use of a spear or a knife than from the use of a stick it must not be assumed that the court takes a lenient view where a stick is used.

But nature of weapon is not viewed in isolation of other surrounding circumstances

CASE: *Salvatorio Ayoo, Joel Ogei v Uganda* Criminal Appeal No. 27/85 (Supreme Court)

The two appellants were indicted together with eight others for the murder of Oruk. On the day before the death of the deceased, A1 went to the home of Achako where there was a drinking party and informed the people that there was going to be a meeting at the home of the deceased at 8 a.m the following day. He told them that he had caught the deceased with herbs for killing people. The following day people gathered at the house of the deceased at the appointed time. The deceased was not at home, he had gone to his garden. A1 and A2 were among the people who gathered. A1 and other people went to the deceased's garden to look for him. They brought him to his home with his arms tied at the back. He was then assaulted by sticks and stones by the crowd and he eventually died on the spot. Evidence was adduced to the effect that during the assault the appellants had made utterances to the effect that the deceased would not live. The appellants also fought off PW1 who attempted to save the deceased and said that he was preventing them from killing the deceased.

The appellants appealed against the conviction on among other things, the ground that no malice aforethought had been established.

The Supreme Court **held** that:

1. It is well established that malice aforethought can be readily inferred from the use of a sharp instrument such as a knife or a spear when directed at a vital part of the body more than the use of a stick or stone. This, however, does not mean that when a stick or stone is used no such inference can be drawn.

2. In the instant case evidence adduced included utterances by the appellants as they beat the deceased, that he would not live and that PW1 was preventing them from killing the deceased. Taking into account the whole evidence, although what was used were sticks and stones, it was obvious that the crowd meant to kill the deceased as a person who practised witchcraft.

Result: Ground of appeal failed.

Use of non-lethal weapon may negative inference of malice aforethought

CASE: *Yoweri Damulira v R,* 1956 EACA 501 (Court of Appeal for Eastern Africa)
The accused was convicted of the murder of a suspected chicken thief whom he beat with a stick causing injuries, which resulted in death. The accused did not dispute that he caused the death of the deceased, but his defence was that he thought he was striking an animal.

According to the defence, while he was asleep in his house at night, he was awakened by hearing the door of the chicken roost being opened. He went outside. Behind a tree about 4 feet from the house he saw a 'bulky thing' and thinking it was an animal he struck it 3 times with his stick. At the third blow the deceased cried out 'Don't kill me. I am Male'. He told the deceased to go and he (accused) returned to his house. After some time he heard the deceased call out. He found the deceased fallen under a tree. The deceased was taken to hospital where he died later in a day. The postmortem disclosed that he had a cut in the scalp one and three-quarter inches long, bleeding over the brain in the right frontal and left occipital regions, bruising on both forearms above and below the elbows and further bruising on the chest.

Accused was convicted of murder – trial judge rejected the appellant's story.

Issue: On appeal, the issue was whether the evidence established beyond reasonable doubt that when he assaulted the deceased, the appellant intended either to kill him or at least to inflict grievous bodily harm.

Held *inter alia*:

The stick which the appellant used in his assault had a diameter varying between about one inch to one and half inches and weighed about one and a half pounds. It was not a lethal weapon. When death is caused by the use of a non-lethal weapon an inference of malice is much less readily drawn than when a lethal weapon is used. Here the deceased was apparently crouching behind a tree and in the darkness it is unlikely that the appellant could have deliberately directed his blows at vital parts of the body. Taking that factor and the nature of the weapon into consideration we think that there is at least a reasonable doubt as to whether the appellant intended to kill or do grievous harm to the deceased. The conviction for murder cannot therefore stand.

CASE: *Mugao and Another v R* [1972] EA 543 (East African Court of Appeal)
Two suspected thieves were beaten with long, thin, green branches to obtain information from them as to the whereabouts of the remains of the goat. One of the suspected thieves died. Two members of the crowd which beat up the victims were convicted of murder.

Court **held** *inter alia* that:

> in view of the weapon chosen, no intention to cause death had been proved. Had the appellants intended to kill they would not have selected light sticks with which to beat the deceased. The intention seemed to be that by inflicting pain, they would obtain information from the suspects.

> The death of the deceased was not a probable consequence of the unlawful purpose of beating with light sticks.

Malice aforethought and the body of the injured person
Malice aforethought inferred from nature of injury inflicted
CASE: In *Uganda v Ochieng* [1992-1993] HCB 80 it was held *inter alia* that:

> Malice aforethought may be summarised as the intentional killing of a human being or knowledge that one's act or omission will probably result in the death of a human being. To establish the existence of malice aforethought court takes into account the following:
> (a) The number of injuries inflicted.
> (b) The part of the body where the injury was inflicted.
> (c) Nature of the weapon used.
> (d) The conduct of the killer before and after the attack.

> In the instant case, striking of the deceased on the lower part of the abdomen which was a vulnerable and sensitive part of the body and the stick used was evidence of evil intention to cause the death of the victim or knowledge that the act would probably cause death.

CASE: *Kalaudio Terikabi v Ug.* [EACA] Criminal Appeal No. 124/1975 (East African Court of Appeal)
The appellant was convicted of murder. The post mortem examination revealed six big cut wounds on the head of the deceased, cut wounds 'digging into the brain' and both hands amputated.

Held *inter alia*:

> The nature of the wounds left no doubt that they were inflicted with the intention of causing death.

Number of injuries, parts of the body assaulted
CASE: *Uganda v Abdu Muherwa* [1972] EA 466

The accused was indicted for murder. It was the case for the prosecution that the accused waited in ambush to catch the thief who had been stealing his beans from the garden. When the deceased came and started uprooting the beans, the accused went and cut him with a panga on the left thigh severing major blood vessels which caused bleeding from which the deceased died. The prosecution contended that the accused had formed a prior intent to kill the deceased.

Held: The accused had not formed a prior intent to kill the deceased as indicated by the number of injuries on the deceased and their positions. One would have expected him to cut the deceased several times and on vital organs or parts of the body such as the head if he had intended to kill him, but not on the leg.

Other proofs of malice aforethought

Post mortem report by itself not sufficient to prove malice aforethought
CASE: *Kanyarutoke v Uganda* Criminal Appeal No.19 of 2001. (Court of Appeal for Uganda)

Kanyarutokye was convicted of murder. The facts of the case are that the deceased was a security guard employed by GFS. The appellant was also employed by the same company as a guard supervisor. The deceased was deployed to guard some premises. The appellant whose duties included patrolling and supervising the GFS guards wherever they were deployed went to check where the deceased had been deployed. He found the deceased drunk and decided to disarm him. A scuffle ensued between the appellant and the deceased as the latter resisted being disarmed. The deceased was injured in the process.

According to the post mortem examination report the deceased had a ruptured spleen with massive haemoperitoneum. The cause of death was put as haemorrhagic shock.

According to the prosecution, malice aforethought could be inferred from the nature of injuries inflicted and the part of the body on which inflicted.

Judgement: In the judgement of the court it was *inter alia* said that:

> A post mortem report by itself is not sufficient to prove malice aforethought beyond reasonable doubt. There is need for other evidence direct or circumstantial on the issue … in this case, taking the evidence on record as a whole, there is no doubt that the appellant was intent to disarm the deceased but not to kill him. …therefore malice aforethought was not proved beyond reasonable doubt.

Result: Accused could not be guilty of murder.

CASE: *Francis Ocoke v Uganda* [1992-93] HCB 43 (Supreme Court)

The appellant was convicted of murder. He appealed against conviction *inter alia* on the ground that the learned trial judge erred in law when on the basis of a post mortem report he held that there was malice aforethought when the appellant killed the deceased.

The Supreme Court held that a post mortem report contains findings as to the state of the body, the injuries found on it, and an opinion as to the cause of death. It is not capable by itself of proving malice aforethought. The existence of malice aforethought is not a question of opinion but of fact to be determined from all available evidence. Therefore the trial judge was not justified in finding that malice aforethought had been established beyond reasonable doubt from the evidence of the medical Doctor in absence of evidence of eye witnesses or circumstantial evidence on the issue.

Malice aforethought: necessary for prosecution to produce weapon in court or to carefully describe it

CASE: *Sentongo v Uganda* [1975] HCB 240 EACA [Law, Ag. P., Mustafa, Ag. V-P & Musoke, J.A)

The appellants were jointly charged and convicted of murder contrary to Section 183 of the Uganda Penal Code. (See page 48 for details of the case)

At the trial the sticks that had been used to beat the deceased were not produced in evidence. However, they were described by witnesses as 'long' and 'slightly big'.

The learned trial judge found malice aforethought clearly established both from the actions of the appellants in wantonly and continually assaulting the deceased with sticks and in the nature of the injuries and their extent.

On appeal it was **held** *inter alia*:
1. Where the deceased is beaten with sticks and the sticks are not produced in evidence, a careful description of the sticks is necessary, if only to assist the trial court in determining whether the instrument allegedly used in a murder case is intrinsically a lethal weapon or not.
2. On the evidence, the sticks used by the appellants were not of a nature likely to cause death nor were they used for that purpose.

CASE: *Thabo Meli v R* [1954] 1 All ER 373, [1954] 1 WLR 228 (Privy Council)
The accused planned to kill the deceased in a hut and thereafter to roll his body over a cliff so that it might appear to be a case of accidental death. The deceased was rendered unconscious in the hut and, believing him to be dead, the accused rolled him over the cliff. There was medical evidence that the deceased was not killed by the injuries received in the hut, but died from exposure where he had been left at the bottom of the cliff.

It was argued that the accused were not guilty of murder because, while the first act was accompanied by *mens rea*, it was not the cause of death, and because the second act, while it was the cause of death, was not accompanied by *mens rea*, the accused believing their victim to be dead already. The Privy Council rejected this argument, holding that the two acts formed part of a series which cannot be divided up. Accordingly the accused were guilty of murder.

Failure to prove malice aforethought: Verdict of manslaughter

CASE: *Sharmpal Singh s/o Pritam Singh v R* [1960] EA 762
Before an accused can be convicted of murder, the evidence must establish beyond reasonable doubt that he intended to cause death or knew that his act would probably cause death.

Where the prosecution is relying on circumstantial evidence, the evidence must exclude all reasonable possibilities save that of guilt.

The circumstantial evidence must eliminate as a reasonable possibility that the appellant did not have such an intention or such knowledge, but caused a great deal more harm than he intended or anticipated.

Common intention in homicides

The issue of common intention in murder arises in cases where a person is killed through an assault by more than one person, sometimes in the furtherance of another crime. Under Section 20 of the Uganda Penal Code,[7] it is provided that:

> When two or more persons form a common intention to prosecute an unlawful purpose in conjunction with one another, and in the prosecution of such purpose an offence is committed of such a nature that its commission was a probable consequence of the prosecution of such purpose, each of them is deemed to have committed the offence.

CASE: *Francis Sebanenya, Petero Kabafumu v Uganda* Criminal Appeal No 17/1989 (Supreme Court)

The Supreme Court provided some guidelines as to when common intention exists:

a) If there is a prior agreement to prosecute the unlawful act or
b) If the accused person or persons are present and participating either physically or by tacit approval in the unlawful act or
c) If the accused person or persons send another person or persons to commit the unlawful act.

CASE: *Kitwala Ronald and 3 Others v Uganda*, Criminal Appeal 70/98 (Court of Appeal)

The four appellants unlawfully arrested the deceased in order to extort money from him. They roughed him up and assaulted him in an attempt to extort the bribe from him. They confiscated his bike for the same purpose.

A2, A3 and A4, all members of the Local Defence Unit (LDU) were armed with guns but A1 was not. A one stage during the 'torture', A1 asked A3 to give him his gun and A3 complied with the request. A1 then fired one shot in the air after which he fired one bullet in the face of the victim. The deceased fell down and A1 fired another two bullets at the legs of the deceased. The deceased died instantly. The four were convicted of murder and they appealed.

Issue: Whether A 2 and A4 had a common intention with A1 to cause death.

The Court of Appeal said *inter alia*:

> All the four men assaulted the deceased. They all took part in demanding the bribe. A2 and A4 had guns but did not use them. Could they have reasonably foreseen that A1 who was a more senior security officer, a corporal and police man, who was not armed, would suddenly get a gun and shoot the deceased?

The Court answered:

> If the two were not members of the Local Defence Unit, our answer would have been in

the negative. Members of the LDU, like police officers have a duty to protect life and property of the people. They should not in the first place have engaged in the unlawful act of extorting a bribe. They had a duty to protect the deceased. They also had the capacity and the opportunity to prevent the first appellant from shooting the deceased. Though he acted rather suddenly, it should be remembered that he was not armed in the first place. He asked for a gun … when they were seeing and hearing. If they had no common intention with A1, this should have alerted them that he was about to do what they had the duty to prevent. They did nothing. Then a gun was handed to him and they did nothing. He must have cocked the gun before shooting but they looked on and did nothing. He first shot in the air … Surely if they did not approve or acquiesce in what he was doing they had enough time to disarm him at any of these stages when it had become clear that he was already so worked up that he could shoot the deceased. Instead, they stood there with their guns aimed at the crowd until the first appellant shot the deceased three times. Even their final act of shooting in the air together as they left the scene clearly was meant to scare the people who would have arrested them. … In the circumstances we have no doubt that all the appellants not only acquiesced and encouraged the commission of the crime but also fully participated in its commission.

Result: Conviction of murder upheld.

CASE: *Salvatorio Ayoo, Joel Ogei v Uganda* Criminal Appeal No. 27/85 (Supreme Court.)

The two appellants were indicted together with eight others for the murder of Oruk. On the day before the death of the deceased, A1 went to the home of Achako where there was a drinking party and informed the people that there was going to be a meeting at the home of the deceased at 8 a.m the following day. He told them that he had caught the deceased with herbs for killing people. The following day people gathered at the house of the deceased at the appointed time. The deceased was not at home, he had gone to his garden. A1 and A2 were among the people who gathered. A1 and other people went to the deceased's garden to look for him. They brought him to his home with his arms tied at the back. He was then assaulted by sticks and stones by the crowd and he eventually died on the spot. Evidence was adduced to the effect that during the assault they had made utterances to the effect that the deceased would not live. The appellants also fought off PW1 who attempted to save the deceased and said that he was preventing them from killing the deceased.

On the issue of common intention, the Supreme Court said:

Evidence was adduced that a meeting was convened at the deceased's home because it was alleged that he practised witchcraft. When the deceased was brought the crowd which had gathered beat him with stones and sticks and he died on the spot. There was no dispute that the decease died of the beatings. The crowd gathered with intent to carry out an unlawful purpose namely to kill the deceased. Under the provisions of Section 22 of the Penal Code, each of them is deemed to have committed the offence. Both appellants were present and did not disassociate themselves from the unlawful act. The 2 appellants were therefore rightly convicted of murder.

CASE: *Tabulayenka s/o Kirya, Garandi s/o Kasaja and Others.* Criminal Appeals 162, 163, 164 and 165 of 1942. (Court of Appeal for Eastern Africa)

The four accused in this appeal were found guilty of murder and sentenced to death. A suspected thief, one Mikairi, was discovered sitting near the door of a hut at night. The alarm was sounded and several persons came rushing to the spot and at once proceeded to belabour Mikairi with fists, feet and such weapons they could lay their hands on. The result was death from multiple injuries.

Evidence indicated that all the four accused took part in the beating in one form or another and in the presence of each other.

The learned trial judge held that Section 22 of the Penal Code Act had no application to the facts. According to him, the case would only be within that section if there was evidence from which it could be inferred that at some time during the night the four accused had formed the intention to assault the deceased in conjunction with one another. Yet the evidence available was that each of the four men answered the alarm and went to the scene independently, each one taking up the assault on the deceased as he arrived.

Held: In reaction to the trial judge's pronouncements, the Appeal Court held:

1. To constitute a common intention to prosecute an unlawful purpose within the meaning of Section 22 e.g. to beat a so-called thief, there being no suggestion that the violence used was necessary to effect the thief's arrest, it is not necessary that there should have been any concerted agreement between the accused prior to the attack on the so-called thief. Their common intention may be inferred from their presence, their actions, and the omission of any of them to dissociate himself from the assault.

2. For the purpose of Section 220 (e)[8], it is not necessary that each of the accused knew that his act or acts would probably cause grievous harm. It is sufficient if the cumulative effect of the beating carried out by the different accused was such as would probably result in death or grievous harm and if all the accused had associated themselves with the assault, as the evidence shows they did, each accused is responsible for all the acts of the others done in furtherance of their common purpose.

Judgement:

We do not agree that Section 22 is not applicable. The fact that the 4 accused answered the alarm and went to the scene independently, each one taking up the assault as he arrived, does not rule out a common intention. Each as he arrived showed by his actions that his intention was at least to beat the thief, and when they were all assembled, the beating in some form or other continued until the deceased died. In these circumstances they were all so identified with the fatal assault on the deceased that they may be said to have formed a common intention to prosecute an unlawful purpose in conjunction with one another, the unlawful purpose being to beat the so-called thief.

Was the common intention merely to beat the deceased or was it something more namely to cause death or to do grievous harm or did each one of them beat or associate themselves with the assault with the knowledge that the beating would probably cause death or grievous harm?

The learned judge said he had no doubt that each of the accused knew that his acts would probably cause grievous harm. This would appear to be so, but it is not necessary to go as far as that. If the cumulative effect of the beating carried out by the different accused was such as would probably result in death or grievous harm and all the accused had associated themselves with the assault, each accused is responsible for all the acts of the others done in the furtherance of their common purpose.

Appeal is dismissed.

CASE: *Defasi Magayi v Uganda* [1965] EA 667

The appellants were convicted of the murder of a suspected thief whom they had beaten with sticks until he died. The evidence was that while suspects were being taken to the Gombolola Headquarters, the second appellant struck the deceased on the head with a stick he was carrying and the deceased fell down. All the other appellants then started beating the deceased and the other two suspects with sticks. During the beating, the second appellant incited the crowd saying 'beat them I will face the case' and the beating continued until the deceased and other died. According to the post mortem report, the deceased had many abrasions on the head, chest and trunk and the left side of his skull had been smashed in and the brain damaged. The cause of death was damage of the brain.

The appellant's appeal to the Court of Appeal failed. The court said at page 670:

> Where a number of persons jointly beat another causing his death and it is not possible to establish which blow actually caused the death, none of the persons taking part in the beating may be convicted of murder *unless* it is proved that he had common intention with the others to kill ...

Held: Having accepted the findings of the trial judge that there was sufficient evidence of common intention against the appellants, the court went on to hold:

> Here was ample evidence of 'common intention'. The unlawful purpose was to beat a so called thief. He was tied up, so there was no question of force being used to effect his arrest. The inference from the actions of all the accused persons in taking part in this unmerciful beating is irresistible – not only did none of the accused persons disassociate himself from the assault but they each prosecuted it with vigour.

CASE: *Uganda v Natseba Lawrence & Others* Criminal Session Case 283/1997 High Court

It was stated that for the doctrine of common intention to operate against an accused, the prosecution does not have to prove that the accused entered into an agreement or made a pact to commit the offence. That the accused was part of the common intention is inferred from his conduct, his presence or actions or from the failure to disassociate, to distance or disengage himself from the commission of the offence. It suffices when it is shown by the actions, conduct and omissions that the accused is acting in concert with others in pursuit of such unlawful purpose to infer that he has formed a common intention with such other persons. If violence is used in achieving such common intention and death of a human being results, then each of the participants will be guilty of murder.

Mob justice and malice aforethought

CASE: *Uganda v Ssenabulya* [1978] HCB 27

Justice Butagira held *inter alia* that it would be difficult to find intention to kill as far as thief beating is concerned where as is invariably the case in the country the participants indulge in it as a game of amusement.

CASE: *Fred Sebanashi v Uganda Criminal* Appeal No. 23/93. (Supreme Court)

The appellant and his co-accused were seen engaged in torturing the deceased. They beat and kicked the deceased interchangeably. They were indicted for murder but both were convicted of manslaughter. The appellant appealed.

Held *inter alia* that it could be inferred from the actions of the two accused persons that they shared a common intention to persecute an unlawful purpose which resulted in the death of the deceased. If they shared a common intention then each of them would be guilty of the offence irrespective of which of them struck the fatal blow.

Interpretation: Where 2 or more people have a common intention to do an unlawful act and death results, each of them is criminally responsible for homicide, irrespective of which of them struck the fatal blow.

Held further that: Where a number of persons jointly beat another causing his death and it is not possible to establish which blow actually caused the death, none of the persons taking part in the beating may be convicted of murder unless it is proved that he had common intention with the others to kill.

Conclusion: In cases of mob justice it is easier to prove that each accused had a common intention to cause injury than to prove that each had a common intention to kill. Therefore it is easier to convict of manslaughter than murder.

Difficulties of proving murder in cases of mob justice can perhaps be explained by what was said in *Uganda v Waiswa and Another* [1977] HCB 300. (High Court)

A1 and A2 went looking for one B whom they suspected of having stolen iron sheets from A's house. Having failed to locate B, the search party went for the deceased (Kamara) who was a renowned thief. The search party dragged the deceased to various places urging him to tell them where B was hiding. As they dragged the deceased along with them they also beat him severely. The deceased eventually died.

The main issues were:
1. Whether the two accused shared a common intention in assaulting the deceased
2. Whether in assaulting the deceased the accused persons shared a common intention to kill or knew that the assault on the deceased would cause death in terms of Section 186 of the Penal Code.

Held:
1. For an offence of murder to be established the common intention must not only be to prosecute an unlawful purpose as is required in S.22 of the Penal Code Act but there must be established the sharing of a common purpose to

kill or knowledge that the act causing death will probably cause death.

2. A common intention to prosecute an unlawful purpose, such as assault per se, where death results amounts to manslaughter.
3. An intention to kill may be formed at the moment of assault; an accused need not have the intention to kill prior to the assault. The intention could be inferred from the weapons used, the actions of the accused persons and the injuries inflicted.

CASE: *Tindira s/o Chiru and Maria s/o Panduji v Rex* Criminal Appeals Nos. 88 and 89 of 1951 (East African Court of Appeal)
The two appellants were convicted of murder before the High Court of Tanganyika. Both accused who were drunk and armed with sticks, intervened in a quarrel over a woman and hit an unarmed man. The first appellant used a heavy stick; the second a piece of thin bamboo. (See page 36 for case details).

The court found no merit in the first appellant's appeal. In the appeal of the second appellant one of the issues was whether his offence was murder or manslaughter. Having found that the appellant could be deemed to have caused death under Section 189 (e), the court said of malice aforethought:

> The malice aforethought could only be established by evidence proving that the appellant when he struck the deceased intended to cause death. Since there was no evidence of common intention, different considerations had to be taken into account in determining the intention of each accused. In the case of the first appellant the heavy weapon and the great force exercised lead irresistibly to the conclusion that he intended to cause death. In the case of the second appellant the weapon used was a thin bamboo stick, and medical evidence was that moderate force must have been used. Had the judge correctly directed himself on the issue of common intent, and considered the degree of culpability of the second appellant separately from that of the first appellant, he would have concluded that the second appellant had no malice aforethought.

Result: Second appellant guilty of manslaughter and not murder.

1. *Primarily* because as will be discussed later, the law sometimes reduces murder to manslaughter even where the killing is done with malice aforethought. [See the discussion on Provocation, Infanticide and Suicide Pacts – homicides often described as voluntary manslaughter].
2. Issues may arise as to whether he can be guilty of manslaughter.
3. An issue may arise as to whether he can be convicted of attempted murder.
4. I am aware that in the celebrated case of *DPP v Smith* [1961] 291, the House of Lords held that intention to cause grievous harm constitutes malice aforethought. Whereas that is in the position in English Law, the East African Court of Appeal and the Ugandan Supreme Court have held otherwise as discussed below.
5. In the celebrated case of *DPP v Smith* [1961] AC 290; [1960] 2 All ER 161 it was held by the

House of Lords that if one has an intention unlawfully to cause grievous bodily harm but he thereby causes death, he is as guilty of murder as a person whose assault was accompanied by an intention to kill. In other words, an intention to do grievous bodily harm is sufficient mens rea for murder. *Bukenya* and *Rujumba's* cases clearly indicate that the law in Uganda is different.

6. The position of the law as established in *DPP v Beard* has been repeatedly restated with approval in several decisions of the East African Court of Appeal, as well as by the High Court and appellate courts in Uganda. See for example *Cheminingwa v R* (1956) EACA 451; *Manyara v R* (1955), 22 EACA 502; *Samuel* Criminal Case No. 243/98.

7. Formerly Section 22.

8. Now 196 (e).

4
Attempt to murder

In criminal law, an attempt to commit a crime is in itself a crime.

Section 204 Penal Code Act:

Any person may be guilty who:
(a) attempts unlawfully to cause the death of another;
(b) with intent unlawfully to cause the death of another does any act, or omits to do any act which it is his duty to do, such act or omission being of such a nature as to be likely to endanger human life, is guilty of a felony and is liable to imprisonment for life.

An attempt to murder is a crime, even if it is unsuccessful. As with the crime of murder, specific intent and malice aforethought also have to be proved.

Malice aforethought is essential in attempted murder
CASE: *Sam Lutaya v Uganda* Criminal. Appeal No. 10/1986. (Supreme Court of Uganda.)
On 26/11/1980, the complainant was with his family inside his house. He heard his bedroom window being banged repeatedly and voices telling the occupants to open. It was a glass window and without curtains. He went to the window and asked the people outside if there was any problem. They told the complainant to open but he refused and raised an alarm. Then two of the attackers, among them the appellant, who had guns at the ready, started firing into the house. Six other members of the group apparently did nothing. The complainant was hit on the abdomen and fell down.

The appellant was convicted of attempted murder but appealed. One of the grounds of appeal was that the prosecution had not established malice aforethought.

Held: Supreme Court held *inter alia*:
- Malice aforethought is an essential element of attempted murder and no lesser intent than that will suffice.
- The appellant's intention to cause death could be inferred from his knowledge that firing the gun would cause the death of the complainant or some other person.

The court also distinguished 'mere preparations to commit the crime' and an attempt thus:
- Where an accused obtains a gun, loads it, goes with it to the place of the intended victim, such conduct constitutes preparation.
- If in addition to the above, the accused aims the gun in the direction of and within the range where the complainant is, and fires the gun, this constitutes attempt to cause death.

Result: The Appeal was dismissed.

Intention to cause grievous harm is not sufficient in attempted murder

CASE: *Rex v Luseru s/o Wandera*

In a prosecution for attempted murder, it is not sufficient to prove that the offence would have been murder if death had ensued; it must be shown that the accused had a positive intention unlawfully to cause death.

An intent merely to cause grievous harm … is not sufficient to support a conviction for attempted murder.

CASE: *Yunusu Mugisa v Uganda.* Criminal Appeal No. 12/94 (Supreme Court)

In a case of attempted murder, malice aforethought must be proved. The prosecution must prove either that the accused intended to cause death (Section 186 (a)) or was indifferent as to his causing death (Section 186 (b)).

According to the court, in the specific case, the lack of medical evidence makes it difficult to infer intention beyond reasonable doubt, together with the lack of any announced intent, the circumstances rendered the case ambiguous as to whether the appellant wanted to kill or frighten his victims.

If malice aforethought is not proved, the accused can be convicted of either grievous harm or unlawful wounding, etc. depending on the nature of the injury sustained by the victim as a result.

CASE: *Sam Lutaya v Uganda* Criminal Appeal No. 10/1986 (Supreme Court)

The appellant Sam Lutaya was with others charged with attempted murder. On the night in question, the complainant was in his house when he heard a bang on his bedroom window. The complainant went to investigate and found men outside the house. Some were armed with guns. The group demanded that the door be opened, as they were security officers searching for illegal weapons. The complainant suspected that the description was false and instead raised an alarm. As he did so, one of the group members shot at him and wounded him in the stomach.

On a conviction of attempted murder, the appellant appealed and one of the grounds of appeal was that:

The necessary *mens rea* in attempted murder was not proved.

The Supreme Court **held** that:

Each case depends on its own circumstances. But if in the attempt to invade a man's house, one of the assailants with common intent discharges a gun at close range at the occupant of a house and in fact wounds that occupant, the intent to kill can readily be inferred.

Result: Appeal dismissed.

5
The Death Penalty in Murder

Section 189 of the Penal Code Act:

Any person convicted of murder shall be sentenced to death.

Once a person has been convicted of murder, the only valid sentence that the court can pass is the death penalty. The sentence for murder is mandatory and the court has no discretion in the matter. Note, however that:

1. Since the death penalty is attached to murder, the High Court is the court of first instance.
2. A person who has been sentenced to death has an automatic right of appeal to the Court of Appeal.
3. Where the Court of Appeal confirms the verdict and consequently the sentence, the accused has an automatic right of appeal to the Supreme Court.
4. It is only if the verdict is confirmed by the Supreme Court that a convict can ever be executed.[1]

Should the death penalty be retained or abolished?

It is noted in the report on the constitution making process[2] that the debate on the need to abolish the death penalty did not receive substantial submissions. Nevertheless, the majority of views submitted supported the retention of capital punishment for a conviction of murder, among other 'serious' crimes.

Arguments in support of retention

Some of the arguments in support of retention of the sentence were as follows:

- Because of long periods of unrest in the country, there are many criminals who fear only death and if capital punishment was removed, such persons are likely to commit wanton murders without fear.
- Although cruel, the death sentence has a deterrent force.
- History has shown that with each change of regime/government, prisoners sentenced to life imprisonment have in the ensuing confusion, escaped from prison and terrorised the populace.
- Many murders in Uganda are committed, not by people with psychological problems but rather by normal people who intentionally kill in order to settle scores with enemies or to eliminate business, political and other rivals, or who are hired to eliminate other people's enemies.
- The death penalty is a clear indication to all that life is sacred and thus whoever takes the life of another must be deprived of life.

Arguments in support of abolition

On the other hand the relatively few submissions which called for abolition of capital punishment supported their view with the following arguments:

- Capital punishment has never served as a deterrent in any society.
- The death penalty is a remnant of the old philosophy of 'an eye for an eye', which was prevalent in pre-modern society, and such a concept of justice should have no place in civilised society.
- Capital punishment is cruel and makes human life cheap. It is premeditated murder by the state and once the state is empowered to destroy life, it may tend to disregard the lives of its citizens.

Recommendations of the Constitutional Commission

Having considered arguments for the retention of the death sentence on the one hand, and for its abolition on the other, as well as global moves towards its abolition, the Constitutional Commission still recommended its retention for murder among other offences. It was argued by the Commission that:

- There was no strong justification for a recommendation that would differ from the majority view.
- That the penalty should not be mandatory and that the relevant court of law should have the discretion to determine whether, in a particular case, the offender should be subjected to the maximum sentence or to a lesser punishment.
- That anyone accused of a crime which carries the death penalty as a possibility should be provided with legal aid by the state.
- That the issue of the death penalty should be regularly revisited through national debates in order to gauge whether public sentiments have over the years changed.

The right to life and the death penalty

World over, the legitimacy of the death penalty is being questioned from a human rights perspective. Even in Uganda there are voices from within civil society which are calling for its abolition. However, as already mentioned above, the Constitutional Commission was not convinced that there was strong justification for a recommendation that would differ from the majority view that the penalty should remain as part of Uganda's criminal law. Consequently the 1995 Constitution retained what was contained in the earlier (1967) Constitution:

> **Article 22(1):** No person shall be deprived of life intentionally *except in execution of a sentence passed in a fair trial by a court* of competent jurisdiction *in respect of a criminal offence* under the laws of Uganda and the conviction and sentence have been confirmed by the highest appellate court. [My emphasis]

A look at the Uganda Penal Code reveals several offences to which the death penalty is attached:

- Treason
- Rape
- Defilement
- Aggravated robbery
- Kidnapping or detaining with intent to murder.[3]

Whereas the penalty is mandatory for a person convicted of treason and murder, it is only the maximum sentence possible in the other mentioned offences. Thus, in those other cases, a judge has the discretion to decide whether to sentence the offender to the maximum or to a lesser sentence.

How does the death penalty appear from a rights perspective?

The legitimacy of the death penalty is increasingly under question. It is considered by many human rights activists as degrading and inhuman treatment. It is often said that the death penalty can no longer pass the test of international standards of basic human dignity. Consequently, there is a world-wide trend towards its abolition.

In 1984, the United Nations General Assembly passed the *Convention against Torture and other inhuman or degrading Treatment or Punishment.*[4]   Under Article 24 of the 1995 Constitution it is provided that 'No person shall be subjected to any form of torture, and, inhuman or degrading treatment or punishment.'

It is argued by some jurists that the execution of a person by whatever means amounts to a cruel, inhuman and degrading act.

The International Covenant on Civil and Political Rights (ICCPR, 1966) provides that: 'anyone sentenced to death shall have the right to seek pardon or commutation of the sentence.'[5]

In 1989, the UN Commission on Human Rights came up with the Second Optional Protocol to the ICCPR, aimed at the abolition of the death penalty. In its General Comment 6, the Commission stated that although state parties are not obliged to abolish the death penalty totally, they are obliged to limit its use, and in particular, to abolish it for other than the 'most serious crimes'. States are enjoined to consider reviewing their criminal laws in this light.

What we note, however, is that in Uganda, the 1990s saw an increase in the number of cases which attract the death penalty. And even the more recently enacted Suppression of Terrorism Act (2001) provides for the death penalty.

During the Constitution making process, the majority of the Constituent Assembly delegates voted to retain the penalty and thus the existence of Article 22 of the 1995 Constitution. Retentionists of the death penalty often use this as justification for the penalty, i.e. that it is still a popular form of punishment in Uganda.

We need, however, to question whether issues of fundamental human rights can ever be founded on public opinion or majority opinion *per se*. In the opinion of jurists like Justice Jackson in *West Virginia State Board of Education V. Barnettee*[6] :

> One's right to life ... and other fundamental rights may not be submitted to vote; they depend on the outcome of no election.

Judicial abolition of the death penalty?

Is it possible to talk of 'judicial abolition of the death penalty' – that is, abolition based not on a constitutional article/statutory position but on a judge's ruling? In a 1995 case, the Constitutional Court in South Africa outlawed the death penalty as cruel, inhuman or degrading treatment or punishment. (*Makwanyare and Mchunu v The State)*

In his judgement, Justice Sachs stressed that:

> Every person shall have the right to life. If not, the killer unwittingly achieves a final and

perverse moral victory by making the state a killer too. Thus reducing social abhorrence at the conscious extinction of human beings.

In the same case Justice Chaskalson summed up the reasons why his country decided to abolish the death penalty thus:

> The rights to life and dignity are the most important of all human rights, and the source of all other personal rights. By committing ourselves to a society founded on the recognition of human rights we are required to value these two rights above all others. And this must be so demonstrated by the state in everything that it does, *including the way it punishes criminals.* This is not achieved by objectifying murderers and putting them to death to serve as an example to others in the expectation that they might possibly be deterred thereby.

His Lordship went on to say that the right to life and dignity 'are the essential content of all rights… take them away, and all other rights cease.'

Perhaps the courts in South Africa found it easier to declare the death penalty incapable of passing the test of basic human dignity because the right to life as exemplified in Article 11 of the South African Constitution is unqualified.[7] Although Uganda's Constitutional definition of 'right to life' is qualified, courts in Uganda can consider how the Hungarian Court has acted. In Hungary, as in Uganda the right to life is qualified to the extent that it may be taken away in execution of a sentence passed in a fair trial by a court of competent jurisdiction.[8] Despite this, the Hungarian Constitutional Court expressed the view that an individual's right to life is the most fundamental of all human rights, and since it is paramount and inherent, such a right cannot be compatible with the death penalty.

Makubuya (2000:240) argues that in Uganda:

> The opinion that the death penalty is a violation of the 'right to life' finds its strength in the provisions of Article 20 of the 1995 Constitution which recognises that the fundamental rights and freedoms of the individual are inherent and not granted by the state. . .

> Construed in the context, Article 20 underlines the fact that the right to life is not a privilege granted to an individual by the state but an inalienable and integral part of a person by virtue of being human. It imposes a duty upon *all* organs of the state to respect, uphold, and promote this inalienable right. This implies that neither a court of law, which is an organ of the state, nor the legislature is capable of condemning a person to death. [*My emphasis*]

Protection from torture, cruel, degrading and inhuman punishment: Is there an exception to this right?

Arguments against the death penalty presented above are to the effect that the death penalty denies the executed person his/her very humanity. In addition, it can also be argued that the death penalty degrades and dehumanises the 'offender'. Under Article 24 of the Constitution:

> No person shall be subjected to any form of torture, and, inhuman, or degrading treatment or punishment.'

Under Article 44 of the Constitution:

> Notwithstanding anything in this constitution, there shall be no derogation from the enjoyment of the following rights and freedoms: (a) freedom from torture, cruel, inhuman or degrading treatment or punishment ...

Since the above right is unqualified, once it is agreed that the death penalty dehumanises the offender, then it should be declared unconstitutional.

One may argue that the contradiction between Articles 22(1) and 24 means that each article stands on its own. But according to Makubuya (2000:246):

> The opening line of Article 44 directly implies its supremacy over anything else written in the Constitution. It clearly shows that the right of an individual not to be subjected to torture, cruel, degrading, or inhuman punishment is paramount and cannot under any circumstances be compromised, any other provision to the contrary notwithstanding. This means that although the death penalty is arguably envisaged by Article 22(1) of the Constitution, it cannot in law be imposed by any court of law ...

Makubuya's argument fits in well with the 'constitutional interpretive principle', proposed by Kirby (1995: 7, 8).[9] According to Justice Kirby:

> ... when interpreting constitutional texts, the text must be construed, as far as possible, to resolve any ambiguities[10] that may exist, in favour of a construction which upholds universal human rights in preference to one which does not. ... where the constitution is ambiguous ...Courts must adopt the meaning which conforms to the principles of fundamental rights rather than an interpretation which would involve a departure from such rights. ... Constitutional law, may sometimes fall short of giving effect to fundamental rights ... the inter-relationship of national and international law, including in relation to fundamental rights, is 'undergoing evolution' ... [I]nternational law is a legitimate and important influence on the development of the common law and constitutional law, especially when international law declares the existence of universal and fundamental rights.

In reference to the apparent contradiction, between Articles 22 (1) and 24, Mukubwa (2000: 153) also stated:

> It is a rule of constitutional interpretation that when two provisions are in conflict, with one provision restrictive of the rights that may be claimed under it and another favourable to them, then the latter is to be preferred.

The debate about the place of the death penalty in civilised society still goes on but as far as the law in Uganda is concerned, it is a lawful sentence. As mentioned above, the Constitutional Commission recommended that the issue of the death penalty should be regularly revisited through national debates in order to gauge whether public sentiments have over the years changed. We now await the outcome of the 2003 Constitutional Review Commission.

---

1. See Article 22 (1) of the 1995 Constitution.
2. The Report of the Uganda Constitutional Commission: Analysis and Recommendations.

3. Treason (Section 23), Rape (Sections 123 & 124) Defilement (Section 129), Aggravated robbery (s.286 (2)) kidnapping or detaining with intent to murder (Section 243).
4. UNGA Resolution 39/46 Dec 10, 1984.
5. Article 6(4)
6. 319 U.S 624, 638 (1943),
7. Everyone has the right to life
8. Section 54 of the Constitution of Hungary provides:

> 1) In the Republic of Hungary everyone has the inherent right to life and to human dignity, and no one shall be arbitrarily deprived of this right.
> 2) No one shall be subjected to torture or to cruel or inhuman or degrading punishment.

9. Kirby is a Justice of the High Court of Australia and Special representative of the International Commission of Jurists and Special Representative of the Secretary Gneral of the United Nations for Human Rights in Cambodia.
10. And I add, contradictions

6
The Defence of Diminished Responsibility

As mentioned in Chapter 1, the law's reaction to a specific homicide depends on the circumstances surrounding the killing. The circumstances affect the punishment attached to the killing. A killing under circumstances described by Section 194 is an example of the categorisation of homicides based on the mental status of the accused.

Section 194 of the Uganda Penal Code Act[1]

(1) Where a person is found guilty of the murder or of being a party to the murder of another, and the court is satisfied that he was suffering from such abnormality of mind (whether arising from a condition of arrested or retarded development of mind, or any inherent causes or induced by disease or injury) as substantially impaired his mental responsibility for his acts and omissions in doing or being a party to the murder, the court shall make a special finding to the effect that the accused was guilty of murder but with diminished responsibility.

The elements constituting the defence are therefore as follows:
1. Abnormality of mind
2. Abnormality arising from specified causes
3. Substantial impairment of mind

What the defence does and does not do
The defence of diminished responsibility first became part of Uganda's criminal law in 1960. It is similar to what was introduced into England by the 1957 Homicide Act. A successful plea of the defence leads to a finding of *'Guilty of murder but with diminished responsibility'*. It therefore follows that it is not a complete defence: it does not lead to an acquittal.

Diminished responsibility and the death penalty
According to Section 194 (3) of the Uganda Penal Code, a person who is guilty but with diminished responsibility is treated in a manner similar to a person under 18 years who has committed an offence to which the death penalty is attached. Such a person is kept in safe custody, pending an order by the responsible minister for the accused's detention under Section 105 of the Trial on Indictments Decree.[2] The defence therefore protects the offender from the death penalty, but it does not protect him/her from a criminal record. Thus Collingwood (1967:160) noted:

> Thus in Uganda, diminished responsibility is not strictly a defence, but rather a procedural bar to the imposition of the death penalty for murder, in the same way as the sentence of death is not ordered in respect of a murderer under the age of 18 years.[3]

Diminished responsibility and manslaughter
A strict interpretation of the law also indicates that homicides under Section 194 do not fall within the category of manslaughter. This differs from the position in England

where a successful plea of the defence leads to a verdict of manslaughter.

Diminished responsibility and insanity

We note that under Section 11, which creates the defence of insanity, it is provided that even if a person's mind is affected by disease, if such disease does not render him/her incapable of knowing the nature of his/her act or incapable of knowing that what he/she is doing is wrong, such person will be criminally responsible for any act or omission.

But, unlike in insanity, a person *can* rely on Section 194 even if the nature of his/her mental abnormality was not serious enough to rob him/her of the ability to know what he/she is doing or the ability to know that he/she ought not to do the act or omission in question.

According to Smith and Hogan (1992:213):

> The test appears to be one of moral responsibility. A man whose impulse is irresistible bears no moral responsibility for his act, for he has no choice; a man whose impulse is much more difficult to resist than that of an ordinary man bears a diminished degree of moral responsibility for his act.

In practical terms, persons who are mad in the popular sense but are excluded from the strict definition of legal insanity as established by the McNaughten Rules of Insanity can rely on diminished responsibility.

Diminished responsibility and premeditation

In *Matheson* [1958] 2 All ER 87, [1958] 1 WLR 474, the CA held that the fact that a killing was premeditated does not destroy a plea of Diminished Responsibility.

Elements of defence

What constitutes abnormality of mind?

As noted by Card, Cross and Jones (1992:140): 'Seriously impaired self-control, though irrelevant to insanity is highly relevant in diminished responsibility.'

CASE: *Byrne* [1960] 2 QB 396, [1960] 3 All ER 1

D strangled a young woman in a hostel. After her death, D mutilated her body. Evidence was tendered to the effect that D, from an early age, had been subjected to perverted violent sexual desires. It was stated that the impulse or urge of those desires was stronger than the normal impulse or urge of sex, so that D found it very difficult or perhaps, impossible in some cases to resist putting the desire into practice, and that the act of killing the girl was done under such an impulse or urge.

The trial judge rejected the defence of diminished responsibility. Byrne appealed to the Court of Criminal Appeal.

Held: On appeal, Chief Justice Lord Parker said:

> 'Abnormality of mind' which has to be contrasted with the time-honoured expression in the McNaughten Rules, 'defect of reason', means a state of mind so different from that of ordinary human beings that the reasonable man would term it abnormal. It appears to us to be wide enough to cover the mind's activities in all its aspects, not only the perception of physical acts and matters and the ability to form a rational judgment

whether an act is right or wrong, but also the ability to exercise will-power to control physical acts in accordance with that rational judgment.

What is abnormality of mind arising from specified causes?

The abnormality of mind must result from one of the causes specified in the section, that is:

- Disease
- Injury
- Arrested or retarded development of mind

Thus as pointed out in *Fenton* (1975) 61 Cr App Rep 261, it was said that abnormality of mind due to hate, jealousy or intoxication is outside the defence.

Card, Cross and Jones (1992:140) states that:

> ... if due to alcoholism of such a degree that either the brain had been injured so that there was gross impairment of judgment and emotional response or, where the brain had not been damaged to that extent, the drinking was involuntary in that the accused was unable to resist the impulse to take a first drink (*Tandy*, [1989] 1 All ER 267, CA; *Inseal* [1992] Crim LR 35, CA) or if an accused had the ability to resist the impulse to take the first drink, but thereafter found it irresistible to go on drinking, his mental abnormality would not be due to disease or injury (or either of the specified causes).

And in *Byrne* above, it was stated that the aetiology of the mental abnormality is a matter to be determined solely on medical evidence.

What constitutes substantial impairment of mind?

The abnormality of mind must have substantially impaired the accused's mental responsibility for his acts and omissions in killing or being a party to the killing.

In *Byrne* the Appeal Court held that:

- 'Mental responsibility for his acts' pointed to a consideration of the extent to which the accused's mind was answerable for his physical acts.
- Whether there was a substantial impairment of the accused's mental responsibility is a question of degree.
- The impairment need not be total, but it must be more than trivial.

In *Simcox* [1964] Crim LR 402, CCA it was held that for a successful plea of diminished responsibility, it must be proved that the difficulty the accused had in controlling his conduct must have been greater than would have been experienced by an ordinary person without mental abnormality in the circumstances in question.

Whether the abnormality was such as substantially to impair his mental responsibility is a question of degree and essentially a question of fact.

Smith and Hogan (1992:213) also clarify that:

> It is not necessary that the impulse on which D acted should be found to be irresistible, it is sufficient that the difficulty which D experienced in controlling it (or, rather, failing to control it) was substantially greater than would be experienced in like circumstances by an ordinary man, not suffering from mental abnormality.

In *Lloyd* [1967] 1 QB 17, [1966] 1 All ER 107n, it was stated that the impairment need not be total, but it must be more than trivial or minimal.

In *Campbell* (1987) 84 Cr App Rep 255 at 259, a doctor testified that an epileptic defendant could be 'vulnerable to an impulsive tendency and therefore occasional impulsive acts'. It was held that there was no evidence of diminished responsibility because, *inter alia*, the witness had not said that the impulse would *substantially* impair responsibility.

Burden of proof for the defence of diminished responsibility

The burden of proof is expressly on the accused:

Section 194 (2) of the Uganda Penal Code

> On a charge of murder, it shall be for the defence to prove that the person charged was suffering from such abnormality of mind as is mentioned in subsection (1).

Although there is no statutory requirement of medical evidence, medical evidence would certainly be the best evidence.

CASE: *Uganda v Ssebuguzi & Others.* [1988-1990] HCB 18
Three men were accused of murder. Counsel for A1 put up the defence of diminished responsibility.

Held *inter alia*: The burden of proving diminished responsibility is upon an accused who pleads it. The accused must prove on a balance of probabilities that:
1. He was suffering from an abnormality of mind.
2. That such abnormality of mind i) resulted by reason of condition of arrested or retarded development of mind or any inherent causes or was induced by disease or injury and ii) was such as substantially impaired his mental responsibility for his acts in doing or being a party to the offence.

CASE: *Ssebakijje John v Uganda* Criminal Appeal No. 6/2000 (Supreme Court)
The appellant was convicted of murder by the trial court and by the Court of Appeal. The conviction was based on circumstantial evidence since no one testified to having witnessed the killing. The evidence accepted by the trial court was that on the material day, the appellant went running from his home to his father and brother (PW4). They tied him up, apparently because he appeared to them to be mentally unstable.

Meanwhile a report was made to the authorities that a person had been killed. The dead body was found on a path near the appellant's house. It had several cut wounds. There was a trail of blood from where the dead body was up to the appellant's home. On the basis of information given by the appellant, the deceased's bicycle and a panga stained with blood were found hidden in a bush behind the appellant's house.

Although some prosecution witnesses testified that the appellant's father had told them that the appellant had a mental problem, and although PW4 testified that the appellant appeared mentally unstable when he ran to them, the defence did not call any evidence on the issue of Diminished Responsibility.

On appeal against conviction, one of the grounds presented by the appellant's counsel was that, the trial court as well as the appellate court were wrong in fact and in law, in failing to find Diminished Responsibility.

Held: The Supreme Court observed that:
1. Diminished Responsibility is a creature of statute, which statute expressly places the burden of proving it, on the defence.
2. The defence in the instant case did not call any evidence on the issue nor otherwise seek to prove that the appellant suffered from such abnormality.
   ... The defence had not attempted to discharge its burden of proof.

The court also noted that the prosecution had not produced any evidence of the mental and physical condition of the appellant at the time of arrest. The court observed that such is the usual practice and is desirable in the interest of justice. Nevertheless, the omission cannot be construed in favour of the appellant since the burden of proof was on him and not on the prosecution.

Result: Conviction upheld.

Notes: Where the evidence available raises the probability that an accused was intoxicated or was provoked or acted in self defence, even where the accused has not specifically pleaded that he was not able to form the specific intention to murder due to alcohol, or that he killed as a result of provocation, or in defence of himself, etc., a court has a duty to consider such defences. This is not so for diminished responsibility and insanity. This is because the law specifically puts the burden of proof on the defence.

But just as it is in the case of insanity, the burden of proof on a plea of diminished responsibility is on a balance of probabilities.

CASE: *Rukarekoha Felex v Uganda* Criminal Appeal No. 12/1998 (Supreme Court) On 24/11/95 the wife of the accused died. The accused went to his mother's house and attacked her with a panga. The accused chased away his sister (PW2) and his sister-in-law (PW3) who saw him cut his mother. When the accused saw people in the neighbour's home where the two women were running to, he stopped the chase and disappeared from the area. The victim died from the injuries inflicted by the accused. The accused was not seen in the area until one and half months after the incident when he was sighted hiding in a maize garden near his home.

The background to the incident was that when the wife of the accused fell ill, he was told by a medicine man that the wife was being killed by his father's spirit. On the fateful day he bought a local brew and took it to his mother whom he told to use the brew to appease the spirit. The mother refused to abide because she was a Christian. The accused went away and when his wife died a few hours later, the accused came and attacked his mother.

In his unsworn statement to the trial court, the accused said he did not know what happened to his mother because at that time his head was not working properly. According to him, he came to his senses after he had been taken to prison and that it was while in prison that he learnt of the death of both his mother and his wife.

On the other hand, the accused's sister and sister-in-law testified that the accused was acting normally, albeit with anger.

Held: In his judgement the trial judge found that all ingredients of murder had been proved. He then considered possible defences. He first ruled that diminished responsibility which had been raised by the defence was not a defence but a factor to consider in sentencing. He then convicted the accused of murder.

First appeal: In the Court of Appeal it was contended that the trial judge ought to have been satisfied that the appellant was suffering from diminished responsibility. The appeal court dismissed the appeal and held that diminished responsibility had not been proved.

Second appeal: On appeal to the Supreme Court the grounds were that:
1. The learned justices erred in law and fact in not finding that the appellant had stated that the 'jamming of the mind' had caused him the effect required in Section 188A of the Penal Code Act.
2. The justices erred in law in stating that it was for the defence to prove the arrested or retarded mind having regard to Section 101 of the Evidence Act. Under Section 101 of the Evidence Act when an accused person sets up a defence, the burden of proof shifts to the prosecution. It was therefore an error for the court to have held that the burden lay on the defence.

Held: The Supreme Court held *inter alia*:
1. It is expressly provided by law i.e. section 188A (2) that it shall be for the defence to prove the fact of abnormality of mind if the court is to make the special finding of guilty of murder but with diminished responsibility. The second ground of appeal thus had no merit.
2. Was there sufficient evidence on which a finding of diminished responsibility could have been based? It had not been established because the defence had not called any evidence to show that the alleged 'jamming' of the appellant's mind had arisen from any of the causes set out in Section 188A. Abnormality of mind is related to the causes mentioned in the section.
3. The accused's claim that he lost control of himself and his senses *per se* cannot be proof of abnormality of mind. It appears to be more consistent with loss of his temper upon his wife's death which he must have blamed on his mother, who, to his mind,   could have prevented it.

Counsel for the appellant submitted that belief in the power of spirits amounted to abnormality of mind which impaired his mental responsibility.

The Supreme Court held that:

Generally, belief in the power of spirits, as in anything else, is a natural process or condition of the mind. It may not be common but it is not abnormal. Diminished responsibility is said to be a state of mind bordering on, but falling short of, the state of insanity.

The Supreme Court also gave guidance on the way the question of diminished responsibility must be handled when raised in a trial on a charge of murder. The court said:

We note that the learned trial judge in holding the view that diminished responsibility is not a defence to murder is not alone. In the law book by Justice Collingwood, the learned author commenting on section 188A states: 'The effect of this section is significantly different from the defence of diminished responsibility in England, which if successful reduces murder to manslaughter. Under the Uganda Code, if the defence proves diminished responsibility ... the court convicts the accused of murder with diminished responsibility, but does not sentence him to death. ... Thus in Uganda diminished responsibility is not strictly a defence but rather a procedural bar to the imposition of the death penalty for murder ...' That view was followed by Justice Allen in *Uganda v John Kankuratire* (1975) HCB 134 ...we think this view is misleading. In the instant case the trial court did not consider the issue in connection with the verdict, but when it came to the sentence the learned judge thought his hands were tied because upon the verdict of guilty of murder the mandatory sentence of death has to be passed. Clearly whether it be called a defence or a bar to the death sentence, where it is proved it leads to legal consequences. It leads to a special finding, namely 'guilty of murder with diminished responsibility'. This is different from a verdict of 'guilty of murder'. Despite the phrasing of section 188A, the law does not envisage that the court would pronounce two verdicts separately in the same case i.e., first that the accused is 'guilty of murder' and later that he/she is 'guilty of murder with diminished responsibility'. Nor in our view does it envisage a 'trial' of the issue of diminished responsibility to be held after the trial and conviction on the charge of murder. Diminished responsibility is an issue of fact. It must be tried with all other issues of fact arising out of the charge. The court's finding on it has then to be embodied in its judgement from which the ultimate verdict is deduced and pronounced.

---

1. Formerly Section 188 A.
2. Section 194 (3)
3. *Criminal Law of East and Central Africa*. London: Sweet and Maxwell. Lagos: African Universities Press.

7
Suicide

Under English common law, suicide used to be an offence – it was regarded as self murder. The Suicide Act of 1961 abrogated the crime of committing suicide. Even in Uganda, the Penal Code is silent on the act of suicide and therefore it is not a crime.

Suicide pacts
Section 195 Penal Code Act[1]

> It is murder to intentionally kill a person, even though the person desired to be killed. The motive of the killing would in such circumstances be irrelevant for purposes of criminal responsibility. If a person (A) causes the death of another person (B) as a consequence of a suicide pact between the two (A) is guilty of manslaughter and not murder.

What is a suicide pact?

According to Section 195 (3) of the Penal Code, a suicide pact means an agreement between two or more persons that they help each other die. The agreement can be that each person kills himself or that one of them (A) first kills the other(s) and then takes his own life. The object of the agreement would be that *all* of them would die. If it is proved that one of the parties to the agreement did not have a settled intention to die, such a person cannot plead suicide pact.

For example, if a group of people hire A to kill them, and A's role is to kill the group but is not to die himself, and A goes ahead and kills the members of the group as requested, A would be guilty of murder.

A suicide pact need not involve a third party. Two or more people can enter an agreement in which they would engage in conduct that would lead to the death of all of them. If any of the parties survives he/she will be able to plead suicide pact, but it must be that her survival was accidental. He/she too was supposed to have died.

The defence of suicide pact therefore only arises where at least one of the parties to the agreement survives but others die. It is the survivor that would plead suicide pact. Were it not for the creation of the section, the survivor would be guilty of murder because he/she would have, through an unlawful act accompanied by malice aforethought, caused the death of a human being. The reason for the failed attempt to die, e.g. whether the survivor is prevented by other people from killing him/herself or because the injury he/she inflicted on him/herself fails to lead to death is immaterial for purposes of the defence.

Burden of proof in suicide pacts

Section 195 (2) places the burden of proving the existence of a suicide pact, on the accused, the person who has been indicted for murder.

CASE: In *Uganda v Rev. Fr Paulo Kabishanga (A1) and Sr. Veneranta Nyakato (A2)* [1978] HCB 69
A1 was a parish priest and A2 a nun in the same parish. A1 got together some girls and

formed a group named 'the Samaritan girls'. This was without the knowledge of his superior, the bishop. Administrative wrangles ensued between A1 and his superior over a number of issues and the plight of the 'Samaritan girls' featured prominently. The climax of this stand-off was the suspension of A1 from priesthood.

A1 then threatened that he was going to hang himself. All the girls 'unanimously said that they were going to wherever he went' and added 'since we have coopertox (a poison brand) in the store. And we want to die with you, not leaving you behind, let us drink it but we must take some bottles and hammer to break down the bottles so as to have small pieces to swallow so as to speed the medicine to kill us quickly.'

The medical evidence was to the effect that although the girls took coopertox, their deaths were expedited by strangulation. This was consistent with A1's extra-judicial statement, part of which said 'So I and A2 because the girls were making so much noise, we helped them to die quickly by putting a rope in each one's neck and pulling it until they were all finished.'

While A2 successfully pleaded compulsion and was acquitted, A1 pleaded the existence of a suicide pact.

Held: Justice Asthana held *inter alia*:
1. A suicide pact means a common agreement between two or more persons having for its object the death of all of them whether or not each is to take his own life. But nothing done by a person who enters into a suicide pact shall be treated as done by him in the pursuance of the pact unless it is done while he has the settled intention of dying in pursuance of the pact.
2. From the evidence, especially of the letters found in A1's house and at the scene of the crime, especially one written by one of the deceased girls, and from A1's extra-judicial statement, it was clear that A1 wanted to kill himself and the girls agreed to die with him. This was clearly a suicide pact between the nine deceased girls and A1, and thus A1 was guilty of manslaughter and not murder; section 188B (1) of the Penal Code.

Attempted suicide: Section 210,[2] of the Uganda Penal Code Act
Whereas suicide is not a crime, the attempt to commit suicide is an offence under Section 203, wherein a person who attempts to kill himself is guilty of a misdemeanour.

CASE: *Kabeni v Republic* [1970] EA503 (High Court of Kenya.)
The appellant pleaded guilty to a charge of attempted suicide and was sentenced to 6 months' imprisonment. After her plea the prosecution told the trial magistrate 'committing suicide is very serious'. And in sentencing, the magistrate said: 'It is a very serious offence to try to kill oneself. I take this offence to be very serious ...'

Held: On appeal Justice Trevelyan held:

The offence is only a misdemeanour. An accused such as the appellant needs sympathy and help rather than punishment. A probation officer's report should be obtained as a matter of course before a person convicted of such an offence is dealt with.

Result: Appeal allowed. Released forthwith.

Aiding suicide: Section 209[3] of the Uganda Penal Code Act

Under Section 209 a person who either procures another to kill himself; or counsels another to kill himself and thereby induces him to do so; or aids another in killing himself is guilty of a felony and is liable to imprisonment for life.

Section 209 is essentially aimed at prohibiting any conduct which involves assisting suicide. It 'covers a variety of situations varying almost infinitely in moral culpability; from D who encourages P to commit suicide for the purpose of inheriting his property, to that of D who merely supplies a deadly drug to a suffering and dying P who is anxious to accelerate the end.'

In England the Suicide Act of 1961 in its Section 2(1) made it a crime to 'aid, abet, counsel or procure' a person to commit suicide.

CASE: In *Attorney-General v Able* [1984] 1 All ER 277, the court was called upon to consider Section 2 (1).

Justice Woolf offered some guidance with respect to the interpretation of the provision. He was of the view that in the ordinary case, in deciding whether an offence has been committed, it is preferable to consider the phrase 'aids, abets, counsels or procures' as a whole, but recognised that circumstances could arise which would justify interpreting part of the phrase in isolation.

The judge went on to make it clear that in order for liability to be established under the section it must be proved that:

1. The accused intended to assist a person to commit suicide.
2. While the accused had that intention, he or she provided some assistance to the person contemplating suicide.
3. The person contemplating suicide was thereby in fact assisted or encouraged in taking, or attempting to take his/her life.

Under Section 209, if a person assists another, but death does not ensue, it may be possible to prosecute both persons: one with attempt to commit suicide and another with procuring suicide.

The Euthanasia (assisted suicide) debate

Euthanasia or 'mercy killing' is assisted suicide in very specific circumstances: it is assisting a person who is terminally ill and/or in intense suffering to die even if he or she can be kept alive for some time longer by medication, etc.

Simply put, the debate going on at the global level is whether a person who is suffering from a terminal illness can legally/lawfully be helped by a doctor to end his/her life. The debate is whether the doctor would under such circumstances be immune from criminal prosecution. It is for this reason that within the debate, euthanasia is defined as:

> ... the process of mercifully ending a person's life, allowing that individual to escape terminal illness or an undignified death.[4]

And Chesterman, S (1998:363) defines euthanasia as follows:

> Euthanasia means the intentional killing of a patient by act or omission, as part of her or his medical care.

Although I can safely state that the debate on euthanasia has not taken centre stage within Ugandan society, the wide coverage that has been given to it at a global level makes it worth a mention in this book. I am keenly aware that euthanasia is a highly controversial and emotive issue, for ethical as well as religious reasons. The purpose of its brief mention here is therefore not to argue for or against its legalisation. It is rather to inform (albeit briefly) the student of law about the raging debate which has now gone as far as the European Court of Human Rights.

Here I will limit the focus of my discussion to what has been termed as *active* euthanasia, meaning direct intervention to end the life of a patient, as opposed to *passive* euthanasia which involves withholding or withdrawing life-prolonging measures to allow a patient to die of natural causes.

Euthanasia and murder

As already discussed above, it is criminal to aid another person to commit suicide. It is also worth noting that according to Section 8 (3) of the Penal Code:

> Unless otherwise expressly declared, the motive by which a person is induced to do or omit to do an act, or to form an intention, is immaterial so far as regards criminal responsibility.

When applied to murder, the effect of Section 8 (3) is that one cannot by pleading that an action in killing (forming an intention to kill) another person was in order to save that person from intense suffering, be excused from a verdict of guilty of murder. A person who kills a loved one, in order to save him or her from intense suffering is as guilty of murder as one who kills a close relative in order to inherit property. What is important is that the conduct engaged in by the accused was *intended* to bring about the death of the deceased; it is irrelevant that the intention was accompanied by a 'noble' cause/ motive.

Arguments against euthanasia

One of the reasons advanced against legalisation of euthanasia is the 'sanctity of life' argument which is to the effect that to sanction intentional killing is fundamentally wrong. It is also argued that although it may be desirable to allow euthanasia in certain cases, the possibility of abuse is too real and it could easily be extended to non-voluntary or involuntary euthanasia. According to this argument, allowing even a limited exception necessarily entails further compromise, either as a matter of logic or practice.

In the English case of *Airdale NHS Trust v Bland* 1993 AC 789 Lord Goff said:

> It is not lawful for a doctor to administer a drug to his patient to bring about his death, even though that course is prompted by a humanitarian desire to end his suffering, however great that suffering may be ... So to act is to cross the Rubicon which runs between on the one hand the care of the living patient and on the other hand euthanasia – actively causing his death to avoid suffering.

At page 867, his Lordship concluded that euthanasia is not lawful at common law. In further support for the slippery slope argument it has been contended:

> We acknowledge that there are individual cases in which euthanasia may be seen by

some to be appropriate. But individual cases cannot reasonably establish the founa .tion of a policy which would have such serious and widespread repercussions ... We believe that the issue of euthanasia is one in which the interest of the individual cannot be separated from the interest of society as a whole. (House of Lords Select Committee on Medical Ethics)

CASE: *Pretty v The United Kingdom* Application no. 2346/02[5] (The European Court of Human Rights)

Principal facts

Diane Pretty was a United Kingdom national, born in 1958 and living in Luton. She was dying of motor neurone disease, a degenerative disease affecting the muscles, for which there is no known cure.

The disease was at an advanced stage; the applicant was paralysed from the neck downwards and her life expectancy was very poor. However, her intellect and capacity to make decisions were unimpaired. Given that the final stages of the disease are distressing and undignified, she wanted to be able to control how and when she died and to be spared that suffering and indignity.

Although it is not a crime to commit suicide in English law, the applicant was prevented by her disease from taking such a step without assistance. It is however a crime to assist another to commit suicide under Sections 2 & 1 of the Suicide Act 1961. Ms Pretty wished to be assisted by her husband in committing suicide, but the Director of Public Prosecutions (DPP) had refused her request to guarantee her husband freedom from prosecution if he did so. Her appeals against that decision were unsuccessful.

The application was lodged with the European Court of Human Rights on 21 December 2001.

Complaints

The applicant complained, under Article 2 of the European Convention, that it is for the individual to choose whether to live and that the right to die is the corollary of the right to live and also protected. Accordingly there is a positive obligation on the State to provide a scheme in domestic law to enable her to exercise that right.

She also complained under Article 3 that the United Kingdom Government is obliged not only to refrain from inflicting inhuman and degrading treatment itself, but also to take positive steps to protect persons within its jurisdiction from being subjected to such treatment. The only effective step available to protect the applicant in this way would be an undertaking not to prosecute her husband if he assisted her to commit suicide.

She further relied on Article 8, arguing that it explicitly recognises the right to self-determination, and Article 9, complaining that the failure to give the undertaking and provide a lawful scheme for allowing assisted suicide violated her right to manifest her beliefs. Under Article 14, she argued that the blanket prohibition on assisted suicide discriminates against those who are unable to commit suicide without assistance, whereas the able-bodied are able to exercise the right to die, under domestic law.

Decision of the Court
Article 2
The Court recalled that Article 2 safeguarded the right to life, without which enjoyment of any of the other rights and freedoms in the Convention would be rendered nugatory or meaningless. It covered not only intentional killing, but also the situations where it was permitted to use force which resulted, as an unintended outcome, in the deprivation of life. The Court had moreover held that the first sentence of Article 2 § 1 enjoined States not only to refrain from the intentional and unlawful taking of life, but also to take appropriate steps to safeguard the lives of those within its jurisdiction. This obligation might also imply in certain well-defined circumstances a positive obligation on the authorities to take preventive operational measures to protect an individual whose life was at risk from the criminal acts of another individual.

In its case law in this area the Court had placed consistent emphasis on the obligation of the State to protect life. In these circumstances it was not persuaded that 'the right to life' guaranteed in Article 2 could be interpreted as involving a negative aspect. Article 2 could not, without a distortion of language, be interpreted as conferring the diametrically opposite right, namely a right to die; nor could it create a right to self-determination in the sense of conferring on an individual the entitlement to choose death rather than life.

The Court accordingly found that no right to die, whether at the hands of a third person or with the assistance of a public authority, could be derived from Article 2. There had therefore been no violation of that provision.

Article 3
It was, the Court noted, beyond dispute that the respondent Government had not, themselves, inflicted any ill-treatment on the applicant. Nor was there any complaint that the applicant was not receiving adequate care from the State medical authorities. The applicant had claimed rather that the refusal of the DPP to give an undertaking not to prosecute her husband if he assisted her to commit suicide and the criminal law prohibition on assisted suicide disclosed inhuman and degrading treatment for which the State was responsible. This claim however placed a new and extended construction on the concept of treatment. While the Court had to take a dynamic and flexible approach to the interpretation of the Convention, any interpretation had also to accord with the fundamental objectives of the Convention and its coherence as a system of human rights protection. Article 3 had to be construed in harmony with Article 2. Article 2 was first and foremost a prohibition on the use of lethal force or other conduct which might lead to the death of a human being and did not confer any claim on an individual to require a State to permit or facilitate his or her death.

The Court could not but be sympathetic to the applicant's apprehension that without the possibility of ending her life she faced the prospect of a distressing death. Nonetheless, the positive obligation on the part of the State which had been invoked would require that the State sanction actions intended to terminate life, an obligation that could not be derived from Article 3. The Court therefore concluded that no positive obligation arose under Article 3 in this context and that there had, accordingly, been no violation of that provision.

Article 8

The applicant was prevented by law from exercising her choice to avoid what she considered would be an undignified and distressing end to her life. The Court was not prepared to exclude that this constituted an interference with her right to respect for private life as guaranteed under Article 8 § 1.

The Court recalled that an interference with the exercise of an Article 8 right would not be compatible with Article 8 § 2 unless it was 'in accordance with the law', had an aim or aims that was or were legitimate under that paragraph and was 'necessary in a democratic society' to attain such aim or aims.

The only issue arising from the arguments of the parties was the necessity of any interference and those arguments had focused on its proportionality. In this connection the applicant had attacked the blanket nature of the ban on assisted suicide.

The Court found, in agreement with the House of Lords, that States were entitled to regulate through the operation of the general criminal law activities which were detrimental to the life and safety of other individuals. The law in issue in this case, Section 2 of the Suicide Act, was designed to safeguard life by protecting the weak and vulnerable and especially those who were not in a condition to take informed decisions against acts intended to end life or to assist in ending life.

The Court did not consider that the blanket nature of the ban on assisted suicide was disproportionate. The Government had stated that flexibility was provided for in individual cases by the fact that consent was needed from the DPP to bring a prosecution and by the fact that a maximum sentence was provided, allowing lesser penalties to be imposed as appropriate. It did not appear to be arbitrary for the law to reflect the importance of the right to life, by prohibiting assisted suicide while providing for a system of enforcement and adjudication which allowed due regard to be given in each particular case to the public interest in bringing a prosecution, as well as to the fair and proper requirements of retribution and deterrence.

Nor in the circumstances was there anything disproportionate in the refusal of the DPP to give an advance undertaking that no prosecution would be brought against the applicant's husband. Strong arguments based on the rule of law could be raised against any claim by the executive to exempt individuals or classes of individuals from the operation of the law. In any event, the seriousness of the act for which immunity was claimed was such that the decision of the DPP to refuse the undertaking sought could not be said to be arbitrary or unreasonable.

The Court concluded that the interference could be justified as 'necessary in a democratic society' for the protection of the rights of others. There had therefore been no violation of Article 8.

Article 9

The Court observed that not all opinions or convictions constituted beliefs as protected by Article 9 § 1. The applicant's claims did not involve a form of manifestation of a religion or belief, through worship, teaching, practice or observance as described in the second sentence of the first paragraph. The term 'practice' did not cover each act which was motivated or influenced by a religion or belief. To the extent that the applicant's views reflected her commitment to the principle of personal autonomy, her claim was a restatement of the complaint raised under Article 8. The Court concluded that there had been no violation of Article 9.

Article 14

For the purposes of Article 14 a difference in treatment between persons in analogous or relevantly similar positions was discriminatory if it had no objective and reasonable justification, that is if it did not pursue a legitimate aim or if there was not a reasonable relationship of proportionality between the means employed and the aim sought to be realised. Discrimination could also arise where States without an objective and reasonable justification failed to treat differently persons whose situations were significantly different.

There was, in the Court's view, objective and reasonable justification for not distinguishing in law between those who were and those who were not physically capable of committing suicide. Cogent reasons existed for not seeking to distinguish between those who were able and those who were unable to commit suicide unaided. The borderline between the two categories would often be a very fine one and to seek to build into the law an exemption for those judged to be incapable of committing suicide would seriously undermine the protection of life which the 1961 Act was intended to safeguard and greatly increase the risk of abuse.

Consequently, there had been no violation of Article 14.

Conclusion: The court unanimously held that there had been:
- No violation of Article 2 (right to life) of the European Convention on Human Rights
- No violation of Article 3 (prohibition of inhuman or degrading treatment or punishment)
- No violation of Article 8 (right to respect for private life)
- No violation of Article 9 (freedom of conscience), and
- No violation of Article 14 (prohibition of discrimination).

---

1. Originally Section 188B.

2. Originally Section 203.

3. Originally Section 209.

4. Alford M. "Euthanasia" at http://www.jmu.edu/evision/archive/volume2/essays/ alford.html. Accessed on 30.09.2003.

5. The Court's judgments are accessible on its Internet site (http://www.echr.coe.int).

8
Voluntary Manslaughter

Generally, any unlawful homicide which is not classified as murder is manslaughter. (Card, Cross and Jones, 1992:206)

In the words of Lord Atkins in *Andrews v DPP* (1937):

> Of all crimes, manslaughter appears to afford most difficulties of definition, for it concerns homicide in so many and so varying conditions ... The law recognizes murder on the one hand, based mainly, though not exclusively, on an intention to kill, and manslaughter on the other hand, *based mainly, though not exclusively*, on the absence of intention to kill but with the presence of an element of 'unlawfulness' which is the elusive factor. [My emphasis]

Card, Cross and Jones continue to explain thus:

> There are two generic types of manslaughter – voluntary and involuntary. A person is guilty of voluntary manslaughter where, although he has killed with malice aforethought, he has done so under circumstances which the law regards as mitigating the gravity of his offence. (1992:206)

The Uganda Penal Code creates various categories of voluntary manslaughter:

1. Killings under Provocation, Sections 192 and 193.
2. Suicide Pacts, Section 195
3. Infanticide, Section 213.

In this book, Suicide pacts are covered in Chapter 8 with other types of suicide. This chapter covers Killings under Provocation, Sections 192 and 193 of the Uganda Penal Code.

The defence of provocation

The defence is created under Sections 192 and 193 of the Uganda Penal Code Act:

Section 192

> When a person, who unlawfully kills another under circumstances which, but for the provisions of this section, would constitute murder, does the act which causes death in the heat of passion caused by sudden provocation as hereinafter defined, and before there is time for his passion to cool, he is guilty of manslaughter only.

Section 193

> 1. The term 'provocation' means and includes, except as hereinafter stated, any wrongful act or insult of such nature as to be likely:
>   (a) when done or offered to an ordinary person; or
>   (b) when done or offered in the presence of an ordinary person to another person.
>   (i) who is under his immediate care; or
>   (ii) to whom he stands in a conjugal,parental, filial or fraternal relation, or in the relation of master and servant, to deprive him of the power of self-control and to induce him to commit an assault of the kind which the person charged committed

upon the person by whom the act or insult is done or offered.
2. When such an act or insult is done or offered by one person–
   (a) to another, or
   (b) in the presence of another to a person –
      (i) who is under the immediate care of that other; or
      (ii) to whom that other stands in any such relation as aforesaid, the
      former is said to give to that other provocation for an assault.
3. A lawful act is not provocation to any person for an assault.
4. An act which a person does in consequence of incitement given by another person
   in order to induce him to do the act and thereby to furnish an excuse for committing
   an assault is not provocation to that other person for an assault.

Legal effect of Provocation

A reading of Section 192 indicates that provocation only arises:

> When a person, … unlawfully kills another under circumstances which, but for the
> provisions of this section, would constitute murder.

The effect of Section 192 is that where a person *intentionally* kills another, but
successfully pleads that her/his unlawful conduct was a consequence of a provocative
act by the victim of the homicide, such person will be guilty of manslaughter and not
murder. *A killing under provocation results into voluntary manslaughter.*

Although the homicide is unlawful, and is accompanied by malice aforethought, the
law takes recognition of human frailty and treats the offender with some degree of
leniency.

The defence of provocation can only arise if what was done would otherwise have
been murder. Provocation is thus a partial defence to a murder charge. It is partial
because even when successfully pleaded, the result is not a complete acquittal but
rather, the accused's criminal responsibility is lessened.

Definition of Provocation

Section 193 defines provocation, inter alia as a wrongful act or insult which is likely to
deprive an ordinary person of the power of self-control and to induce him to commit
the kind of assault which he committed upon the victim; the person who had provoked
him.

Provocation therefore refers to the Commission of the offence in the heat of passion
arising from loss of self-control. The offended person must have lost control as a direct
result of an unlawful act committed by the victim.

Cases and rulings on the definition of provocation

In the classic English case of *Duffy* [1949] All ER 932, Justice Devlin said :

> Provocation is some act, or series of acts, done by the dead man to the accused, which
> would cause in any reasonable person, and actually causes in the accused, a sudden
> and temporary loss of self-control, rendering the accused so subject to passion as to
> make him for the moment not master of his mind.

In *Obong Richard s/o Ocen v Uganda* Criminal Appeal 4/82, the Court of Appeal for
Uganda held *inter alia* that:

For the defence of provocation to succeed it must be shown that a normal person was no longer acting normally because he had lost his sense of proportion in the face of provocation.

In *Mancini v DPP* [1942] A.C. 1 the House of Lords held *inter alia* that:

It is not every provocation[1] that will reduce the crime of murder to manslaughter. To have that effect the provocation must be such as temporarily to deprive the person provoked of the power of self-control, as the result of which he commits the act which causes death.

Note: Provocation as a defence can only be pleaded on a murder charge. It is not a defence to lesser offences, such as non-fatal assaults. In *Cunningham* [1959] 1 QB 288, [1958] 3 All ER 711, it was held that legal provocation is not a defence to a charge of unlawful wounding.

Provocation is a question of fact

In Chacha s/o Wamburu v R [1953] 20 EACA 339, it was held *inter alia* that the question of provocation is ordinarily one of fact. Cases below demonstrate who is responsible for proving the fact.

Burden of proof in provocation

CASE: *Joseph Magezi v Uganda* Criminal Appeal No.15/1989
Held: Supreme Court held *inter alia* that:

- An accused does not have the duty of proving provocation, he only has the duty of raising that defence on a balance of probabilities
- Once the defence raises any defence, it is the duty of the prosecution to negative the defence.
- Where evidence adduced shows that the case was as likely to be a case of provocation as not, the benefit of doubt is in favour of the accused.

CASE: *Doto s/o Mtaki v R* [1959] EA 860 (East African Court of Appeal)
The appellant who was convicted of the murder of his wife had admitted killing her but had contended that he was provoked by her. The provocation consisted of refusal to cook a meal and vulgar abuse by the deceased. The trial judge directed the assessors that it was for the appellant to establish probability of provocation and further put this issue to the assessors on the basis that the provocation should be such as to negative an intent to kill. Legal provocation had not been established.

Held on appeal:
Except where there is a plea of insanity, there is no burden on an accused to establish his defence.

CASE: *Uganda v Sempija Samuel* HC Criminal Case No. 243/98
The accused was indicted for murder. He did not put forward provocation as a plea. However, the trial judge held inter alia:

Provocation was not put forward as a plea by the accused. The court is however duty bound to examine it. It is trite law that the burden is never on the accused to establish a plea of provocation. If the evidence discloses a possible plea of provocation, the burden of proof remains throughout on the prosecution to negative it and prove beyond reasonable doubt that the accused did not kill the deceased in the heat of passion caused by sudden provocation.

Nevertheless, the accused does not say that he was ever provoked by the deceased. Indeed the exchange of words between the accused and deceased cannot amount to provocation. The plea of provocation is therefore not open to the accused.

CASE: *Kabengi v Ug.* [1978] HCB 216. Court of Appeal for Uganda.
The appellant was convicted of the murder of Philipo. The appellant testified that the deceased struck him with a burning piece of firewood, and caused him bruises on the shoulder. (The bruises were consistent with the evidence of the medical examination of the appellant.)

Thereupon, the appellant picked a panga thinking it was a stick and struck the deceased once. The prosecution did not attempt to explain the injuries on the appellant in any other way.

In his submission to the assessors, the learned trial judge, directed them that the appellant had committed either murder or nothing, and did not put to them the other defences which emerged from the appellant's evidence although the appellant did not put them forward.

Held *inter alia*:
1. It is the duty of the trial court to deal with all the alternative defences, if any, if they emerge from all the evidence as fit for consideration, notwithstanding that they are not put forward or raised by the defence, for every man on trial for murder is entitled to have the issue of manslaughter left to the assessors if there is evidence on which such a verdict can be given, to deprive him of this constitutes a grave miscarriage of justice – *Mariani v DPP* [1942]A.C
2. The summing up of the assessors was incurably defective in so far as it treated the case as one of murder or nothing and in so far as the judge did not direct the assessors and himself on the effect of the use of excessive force in exercising the right of self defence which renders the offence committed manslaughter. *Moreover, in almost all cases the element of self defence may and does often merge into the element of provocation.* In the result, there was from the evidence, such other alternative defences which ought to have been put to the assessors for consideration, albeit not raised by the appellant. [My emphasis]
3. ... the evidence was consistent with the fact that the appellant must have been provoked...

CASE: *Uganda v No. UD 1131 Sgt. Kelly Omuge alias Rashid alias Tito Lumumba and Baduru Walakira Nyanzi.* Criminal Session Case 95/1985 (High Court)
The court cited *Festo Shirabu s/o Musungu v Regina* Criminal Appeal 72/1955 with approval and said:

> Facts relied on as provocation do not have to be strictly proved. It is only necessary that there should be such evidence as to raise a reasonable probability that they existed. If

this is the effect of the evidence then the onus lying on the prosecution is not discharged.

CASE: In *Yokyadi Lakora s/o Omeri v R* [1960] EA 323[2]
It was stated that in determining provocation, each case must depend on its own facts and the question in each case is whether or not upon the facts of the particular case, the killing was done (or there is a reasonable doubt that it may have been done) in the heat of passion caused by sudden provocation.

Provocation and self-defence

CASE: The judgement in the case of *Uganda v Lukasi Omondi*, Criminal Session Case No. 485/1971 brings out the link between provocation and self-defence. (Before Justice Saied)
The accused was indicted for murder. The accused was chased by a number of people on suspicion that he was a thief. He slashed the deceased, who was one of the chasers, to death.

Held:

1. The chase of the accused on mere suspicion that he was a thief was unlawful. The unlawful chase quite clearly gave rise to provocation and the right to preserve one's freedom, which was being threatened.

2. As the deceased was, however, an old man, the accused could quite easily have brushed him aside instead of hacking him to death. The accused used excessive force in the circumstances. But where elements of both provocation and self-defence existed in a case, and the inference of malice aforethought was rebutted by the circumstances, as was in this case, it mattered little whether the acts be regarded as done in excess of self-defence or under the stress of provocation.

CASE: *Uganda v Ojok* [1992-1993] HCB 54 (High Court)
It is trite law that in determining whether provocation exists, the circumstances be considered from the point of view of the accused.

Legal provocation does not mean absence of malice aforethought
If a person in the heat of passion unlawfully kills another, as a consequence of being provoked by that other person, such killing is treated as 'manslaughter only, in spite of the existence of malice aforethought.'

Cases and rulings on the defence of provocation
In *Doto s/o Mtaki v Regina* Criminal Appeal No 192/1959 the East African Court of Appeal held that:

> …it is not the law in East Africa that, for the defence of provocation to succeed, it must appear that the accused was so provoked as to be incapable of forming an intent to kill or cause dangerous harm.

> …There is no reference in the definition to the question of the capacity or otherwise of the accused to form an intent.

> A killing may be manslaughter in spite of an intention to kill if the intention was formed

and executed in the heat of passion. For the defence of provocation reduces to manslaughter what would otherwise be murder, that is to say, a killing with malice aforethought, one kind of malice aforethought being an intention to kill.

Chacha s/o Wamburu v Rex [1953]20 EACA 339

In answer to the question whether intention to kill necessarily negatives the defence of provocation, the EACA said that 'the mere existence of an intention to kill or inflict grievous harm ... would not of itself deprive an accused of provocation.'

Held: *inter alia* that:

> There is no rule of law that intentional killing precludes a finding of manslaughter only. Malice aforethought, if not 'precedent' but caused by provocation, will not necessarily lead to a finding of murder.

See also *Uganda v Nambwegere s/o Rovumba* [1972] ULR 15 where it was also held that there is no rule that an intention to kill deprives the accused of a defence of provocation.

R v Luseru Wandera [1948]15 EACA 105

It was held that provocation to succeed as a defence, the retaliation must be in the heat of passion, but the existence at such time of an intention to kill does not necessarily negative the defence of provocation.

Provocation requires a subjective as well as an objective test

In considering the question of provocation, it is necessary to apply both a subjective and an objective test: did the provocation in fact cause the accused to lose his power of self control, and could a reasonable person so provoked have lost self control and acted as the accused did?

Definitions

An objective test seeks to determine what a reasonable person would have believed or done and then gauges the behaviour of the accused against that objective or minimal standard. The objective element in the defence of provocation requires that there be a wrongful act or insult of such a nature that it would be sufficient to deprive an ordinary person of the power of self-control.[3]

A subjective test involves an inquiry into what the particular accused believed, intended or knew at the time in question. The subjective element of the defence of provocation requires that the accused respond to the wrongful act or insult before there is time for his or her passion to cool. Once the jury has established that the provocation in question was sufficient to deprive an 'ordinary person' of the power of self-control, it must determine whether that was indeed the case for the accused. At this point [it is necessary to] take into consideration the mental state of the accused, as well as psychological temperament, in order to determine if he or she was in fact acting in response to provocation.[4]

The test of an ordinary and/or reasonable person

For a person to successfully plead provocation, it must be proved that any other ordinary person in the position of the accused would have lost self control and reacted as the accused had acted. Although the section refers to an 'ordinary' person, the interpretation attached to the phrase by the courts is identical to that attached to 'reasonableness' in the defence of self-defence.

In *Mancini v DPP* [1942] A.C. 1, the House of Lords said *inter alia* that in considering whether an accused would be entitled to the defence of provocation, the test to be applied is that of the effect of the provocation on a reasonable man, so that an unusually excitable or pugnacious person is not entitled to rely on provocation which would not have led an ordinary person to act as he did.

In *DPP v Camplin* [1978] 2 All ER 168 Lord Diplock stated that the public policy underlying the adoption of the 'reasonable man' test in the common law doctrine of provocation was to 'reduce the incidence of fatal violence by preventing a person relying on his own exceptional pugnancy or excitability as an excuse for loss of self-control.'

In *Stingel v R* (1990) 171 CLR 312 it was stated by the High Court of Australia that the rationale of the objective test is as follows:

> The objective standard, therefore, may be said to exist in order to ensure that in the evaluation of the provocation defence there is no fluctuating standard of self-control against which accuseds are measured. The governing principles are those of equality and individual responsibility, so that all persons are held to the same standard notwithstanding their distinctive personality traits and varying capacities to achieve the standard. ... however that does not mean that the objective test was intended to be applied in a vacuum or without regard to such of the accused's personal characteristics, attributes or history as serve to identify the implications and to affect the gravity of the particular wrongful act or insult.

Cultural background of accused is relevant

Yovan v Uganda [1970] EA 405

The East African Court of Appeal held that provocation must be judged by the standard of an ordinary person of the community to which the accused belongs. What might be a deadly insult to a member of one community might be a mere triviality to members of another community.

In order to prove that the particular conduct of the deceased would have provoked any other member of the accused's community:

- The prosecution can lead evidence as to the nature and meaning of the particular wrongful act or insults, etc. and as to any relevant custom.
- The court can be guided by the assessors, who presumably have knowledge of the customs of the people.

Even in *R v Hussein* above, the East African Court of Appeal acknowledged the significance of culture, and class in determining whether the accused's action was reasonable and held *inter alia* that:

> The standard of the reasonable man is the reasonable man within the cultural background

of the accused. ...where the wrongful act or insult is of such a nature as would be likely to deprive an ordinary person of the class to which the accused belongs of the power of self-control, there is provocation within the meaning of the statute...

In *R v Fabiano Kinene & Others* (1941) 8 EACA 96 it was held that:

The ordinary person whose standard of behaviour is taken as the test of justifiableness of the accused's reaction, must be considered to be an ordinary person of the same community as the accused himself.

Accused's age is relevant

CASE: *Director of Public Prosecution v Camplin* [1978]2 All ER 168 (House of Lords)

A 15 year old boy killed a man. His only defence was provocation. Held *inter alia* that the proper test is whether the provocation was enough to have made a reasonable person of the age as the appellant in the same circumstances do as he did. The applicable test is what a reasonable 15-year-old boy would have done in the circumstances.

The same view was expressed in the unanimous judgement of the High Court of Australia in *Stingel v R* (1990) 171 CLR 312 at 330, with reference to age in the sense of immaturity, when it was said that ' the approach may be justified on grounds other than compassion, since the process of development from childhood to maturity is something which, being common to us all, is an aspect of ordinariness.'

Note: The Court recognised the importance of the age of the offender in determining the reasonableness of an act.

Sex of the offender is relevant

In *DPP v Camplin* Lord Diplock stated that:

... for the purpose of the law of provocation *the reasonable man has never been confined to the adult male. It means an ordinary person of either sex,* not exceptionally excitable or pugnacious, but possessed of such powers of self-control as everyone is entitled to expect that his fellow citizens will exercise in society as it is today ... the reasonable man referred to in the question is a person having the power of self control to be expected of an ordinary person of the sex and age of the accused, but in other aspects sharing such of the accused's characteristics as would affect the gravity of the provocation to him...

Relevance of physical characteristics

CASE: *Bedder v Director of Public Prosecutions* [1954] 2 All ER 801 (House of Lords)

The appellant, who was sexually impotent, attempted in vain to have intercourse with a prostitute, who jeered at him and hit and kicked him. He then stabbed her with a knife and killed her. He pleaded that there had been provocation by the deceased and that therefore he was guilty of manslaughter and not murder. The trial judge convicted him of murder. He appealed on the ground of misdirection as to the test to be applied in determining whether there was provocation. According to the appellant's argument, in considering the reaction of the hypothetical reasonable man to the acts of provocation, it is necessary that members of the jury place the hypothetical reasonable man in the circumstances in which the accused was, and also invest the reasonable man with the personal physical peculiarities of the accused, as in the present case with the characteristic of impotence, and the question should be asked: what would be the reaction of the impotent reasonable man in the circumstances?

The trial judge had summed up the test of provocation as follows:

> Provocation would arise if the conduct of the deceased woman to the prisoner was such as would cause a reasonable person, and actually caused the person to lose his self-control suddenly and to drive him into such a passion and lack of self-control that he might use violence of the degree and nature which the prisoner used here.

> … The reasonable person, the ordinary person, is the person you must consider when you are considering the effect which any acts, any conduct, any words, might have to justify the steps which were taken in response thereto, so that an unusually excitable or pugnacious individual, or a drunken one or a man who is sexually impotent is not entitled to rely on provocation which would not have led an ordinary person to have acted in the way which was in fact carried out. There may be, infirmity of mind and instability of character, but if it does not amount to insanity, it is no defence. Likewise infirmity of body or affliction of the mind of the assailant is not material in testing whether there has been provocation by the deceased.

Reacting to the above summation of the trial judge, the House of Lords said:

> It appears to me (as it appeared to the trial court) that: No distinction is to be made in the case of a person who, though it may not be a matter of temperament is physically impotent, is conscious of that impotence, and therefore mentally liable to be more excited unduly if he is 'twitted' or attacked on the subject of that particular infirmity.

The House of Lords further stated that:

> It would be illogical not to recognise an unusually excitable or pugnacious temperament in the accused as a matter to be taken into account but yet to recognise for that purpose some unusual physical characteristic, be it impotence or another. Moreover, the proposed distinction appears to ignore the fact that the temper of a man which leads him to react in such a way to provocation is, may be, itself conditioned by some physical defect.

The House of Lords was also of the view that if the reasonable man was invested with the peculiar characteristics of the accused, this would make nonsense of the test. That since the test is to make reference to a certain standard or norm of conduct and thereby invoke the reasonable, average or normal man, if the reasonable man was deprived in whole or part of his reason, or the normal man endowed with abnormal characteristics, the test would cease to have value. It is precisely this that led to the exclusion of an unusually excitable or pugnacious person from relying on provocation.

Result: Appeal dismissed.

What is heat of passion?

In *Yovan v Uganda* [1970] EA 405 the East African Court of Appeal made reference to the phrase 'heat of passion' used in Section.187 (now 193) and held *inter alia* that:

> heat of passion required refers not only to a state of anger but to any emotional state

caused by the provocation and which is such as to deprive an ordinary person of self-control.

In the judgement of the court read by Justice Duffus, it was said:

> It has been suggested in some of the previous cases that the heat of passion refers only to a state of anger. We think that this might be too narrow an interpretation; the intention of the section is to denote an emotional state which has been caused by the act of the person assaulted and is such to deprive an ordinary person of self-control. ... in certain circumstances it would be difficult to say if an appellant acts partially in desperation or in sudden fear or whether he acts wholly in anger. The main element is the sudden reaction which causes such an over powering emotion as to deprive the appellant of self-control.

Immediate retaliation, no time for passion to cool

To successfully plead provocation the offender must have reacted immediately after the provocation, without having had time to cool from the passion caused by that provocation.

As stated by the House of Lords in *Mancini v DPP* [1942] AC 1:

> In deciding whether or not an accused is entitled to the defence of provocation, regard must be had to the time which elapsed between the provocation offered by the deceased and the act of the accused which caused death. It is important to consider whether sufficient interval elapsed (between the provocation and the fatal assault) to have allowed a reasonable person to cool. Furthermore, regard must be had to the offender's conduct during that interval and to all the other circumstances tending to show the state of mind of the accused.

In *Yovan v Uganda* [1970] EA 405, Justice Duffus noted that the main element in provocation is the sudden reaction which causes an overpowering emotion as to deprive the appellant of self control.

In *Duffy* [1949] All ER 932, Justice Devlin said that for a person to successfully plead provocation, there must be 'a sudden and temporary loss of self-control, rendering the accused so subject to passion as to make him for the moment not master of his mind.'

CASE: *Uganda v Yowana Baptist Kabandize* [1982] HCB 93. High Court
The accused and deceased first exchanged unpleasant words and almost fought in a bar. Afterwards, the accused left and went away for half an hour. He changed his attire, got a spear without a handle and rejoined the accused. He came into the bar concealing his spear in his armpit and covering it with a coat. He then walked to the deceased, got the spear from his armpit and stabbed the deceased on the chest and stomach three times. Accused ran outside but did not get back to his home. On arrest he admitted having killed the deceased but said that the deceased had threatened to burn him in his house that night together with his family. This threat was made two nights before the assault on the deceased.

Held *inter alia*:
The defence of provocation was not available to the accused as the threat uttered by

the deceased to burn the accused and his family did not fall within the definition of provocation in Sections 187 and188 (now 192 and 193). The charge of murder would be reduced to manslaughter if the killing was done in the heat of passion and if caused by provocation of a sudden kind and there is no time to cool. In this case, the threat was uttered 2 days before the slaying of the deceased, therefore, there was ample time within which the accused could report to police and cool the temper down. There was no evidence that there was any threat uttered within the bar.

Whether or not a person had time to cool his passion is a question of fact
CASE: *Maina Thuku v Republic* [1965] EA 496 (East African Court of Appeal)
The appellant saw his stepfather, the deceased, beating his mother outside their house when he arrived there in a drunken state one night and tried to separate them. The deceased hit the appellant with a stick twice and told him not to interfere in a fight between husband and wife. The appellant then went into the house and slept for a few hours until he was awakened by the deceased calling him. Upon going outside he found his mother dead with a severe injury at the back of her head and saw the deceased some distance away. The appellant then lifted the body of his dead mother and put it in the shade and then took a panga from the house and chased the deceased to a house about three hundred yards away. There the appellant and the deceased exchanged words which apparently made him more angry and while they were walking towards his mother's body the appellant attacked the deceased and killed him.

The appellant was charged with murder and the trial judge accepted the defence that there was sufficient provocation to have caused the appellant to be in 'the heat of passion'. He however held that that sufficient time had elapsed for the appellant's anger to have subsided and that therefore the plea of provocation could not be sustained.

Held: On appeal, it was held by the East African Court of appeal that:
1. The events were so continuous as to make the act of killing the mother so proximate to the appellant as constructively to have been done in his presence;
2. The degree of provocation is a relevant factor in considering whether the heat of passion in an accused person, regarding him from the standard of the ordinary man, had had the time to cool or whether the provocation would still be bearing on his mind so as to deprive him of the power of self control.
3. When the appellant killed the deceased he was still acting in the heat of passion without regaining his self control; accordingly the plea of provocation was available to the appellant and the conviction of murder should be reduced to manslaughter.

Judgement:
In its judgement, the Court of Appeal said *inter alia*:

> ... We regard the series of incidents here, the beating of the appellant's mother, the assault on the appellant, and the comparatively short sleep of the appellant and his being aroused by the deceased a few hours later in the early morning and his going out and suddenly finding his mother dead, with severe injuries and blood stains, and seeing the deceased going away, as all forming one connected series of events which culminated in his finding the dead body of his mother with injuries which, he correctly concluded,

had been given by the deceased. We think this makes the actual killing of his mother so proximate to the appellant as constructively to have been in his presence ... this was sufficient sudden provocation within the meaning of (the section) to have caused the appellant to get in such a heat of passion as would be sufficient to reduce his crime committed during such a state of mind from murder to manslaughter.

... It is difficult to imagine greater provocation than that of a son witnessing his mother being beaten to death ... the discovery of the dead body and the assault of the deceased was again apparently a continuous series of events, all within a comparatively short period of time. There was the discovery, the chase of the deceased, the passage of words between them and then the final assault which resulted in the death of the deceased. This is a question of fact ...

Heat of passion versus the slow burn

As indicated in the various cases discussed above, a strict interpretation of the law would imply that a successful plea of provocation necessitates that the offender must have reacted immediately after the provocation, without having had time to cool from the passion caused by that provocation. Research on victims of prolonged abuse indicates that such victims sometimes act violently towards their abusers and even kill them, not during an abusive incident, not in the fury of a violent assault but in the aftermath of a row.

Strictly speaking, such a homicidal offender cannot plead provocation. A history of violence against the offender by the deceased cannot of itself be taken as having provoked the offender. The accumulated violence would not of itself reduce the offender's criminal responsibility for the homicide.

However some quarters are in favour of expansion of the time element in order to take into consideration the slow-burning effects of prolonged and severe abuse. This is of particular concern for advocates of the rights of battered women who kill their abusive spouses in self-defence but with excessive force.

The heat of passion: Cases and rulings

In *Luc Thiet Thuan v R* [1996] 2 All ER 1033 the Privy Council *inter alia* said that:

> [I]t may be open to a defendant to establish provocation in circumstances in which the act of the deceased, though relatively unprovocative if taken in isolation, was the last of a series of acts which finally provoked the loss of self-control by the defendant and so precipitated his extreme reaction which led to the death of the deceased. That such a series of events might cumulatively constitute provocation was the opinion expressed by Gibbs J in *Moffa v R* (1977) 138 CLR 601 at 616, cited with approval by the High Court of Australia in *Stingel v R* (1990) 171 CLR 312 at 326.

In *Stingel v R* (1990) 171 CLR 312 (High Court of Australia) it was said that conduct which may in some circumstances be quite unprovocative may be intensely so in other circumstances. Particular acts or words which may, if viewed in isolation, be insignificant may be extremely provocative when viewed cumulatively.

In *Moffa v R* , (1977) 138 CLR 601 (High Court of Australia), where the deceased's insulting conduct had culminated in the throwing of a telephone at the appellant, Justice

Gibbs commented at 616:

> However, it is no doubt right to infer that the throwing of the telephone was only the last straw that caused the applicant's control to collapse. In any case in deciding whether there is sufficient evidence of provocation, it is necessary to have regard to the whole of the deceased person's conduct at the relevant time, for acts and words which considered separately could not amount to provocation may in combination, or cumulatively, be enough to cause a reasonable person to lose his self-control and resort to the kind of violence that caused the death.

CASE: There is also the Ugandan case of *Sofia Auma* HCC SC No. 77/91. High Court. The deceased was husband to the accused (Sofia). The deceased used to subject his wife to severe beatings whenever she refused to give him money for gambling. On the day before the homicide, the accused was subjected to such beating. She reported the matter to the village court. The court could not hear the case on that very day but fixed its hearing for the following day. On that day, before the court could sit, the husband again subjected the accused to severe beating. That very day, the accused served her husband with poisoned food and he died.

Although the period between the assault and the poisoning was long, the court convicted the accused of manslaughter. The court took into consideration the submissions of the defence counsel that the accused and the deceased had had a very unhappy marriage frequented by assaults on the accused by the deceased.

Mode of retaliation must be proportionate to the provocation
Use of weapon in retaliation
The defence of provocation does not mean that any degree of force or any type of weapon will be considered appropriate.

Cases and rulings on the use of a weapon
In *Mancini v DPP* [1914]3 KB 116 it was held, *inter alia*:

> In deciding the question whether legal provocation can be pleaded, regard must be had to the nature of the act by which the offender caused death. Account must be taken of the instrument with which the homicide has been effected. The mode of resentment must bear a reasonable relationship to the provocation if the offence is to be reduced to manslaughter. To justify the use of a lethal weapon the circumstances must indeed be grave.

In *Rex v Lesbini* [1914]3 KB 116 it was held that in determining whether there was legal provocation, it is of particular importance to take into account the instrument with which the homicide was effected, for to resort, in the heat of passion induced, by a simple blow, is a very different thing from making use of a deadly instrument like a concealed dagger. In short, the mode of resentment must bear a reasonable relationship to the provocation if the offence is to be reduced to manslaughter.

Where the mode of retaliation is excessive, a murder verdict may be given and just as it is with self-defence (see below), an unreasonable degree of retaliation to provocation will exclude the defence of provocation.

One could conclude that where a deadly weapon is used in retaliation, the provocation must be great indeed if the offence is to be reduced from murder to manslaughter under Section 192.

CASE: *Marwa s/o Robi v R* [1959] E.A 660

The appellant was convicted of murder for spearing to death the deceased after a dispute over cattle which the deceased claimed and had gone to the appellant to collect. (See page 2 for details of the case.) The trial judge had found that no force was used against the appellant, although the deceased had carried a stick when he went towards the appellant's boma. On appeal, it was argued for the appellant that the trial judge had erred in finding that there was no sufficient provocation to reduce the offence to manslaughter.

Issues:
1. Whether killing in defence of property justified (Section 15 Uganda Penal Code)
2. Whether sufficient provocation to reduce charge of murder to manslaughter.

Held:
1. It must be a question of fact in each case whether the degree of force used in defence of property which caused death was, in the particular circumstances of the case, justifiable, or, if not justifiable, whether it was such as to amount only to manslaughter, or was so excessive as to constitute the offence of murder.
2. In driving off the cattle the deceased was no doubt committing a tresspass, but the means adopted by the appellant to resist the taking of the cattle were utterly out of proportion to the tort which was being committed.
3. The court was satisfied that the trial judge had adequately dealt with the question of provocation and saw no reason to differ from his conclusion.

Result: The verdict of murder was upheld.

Per curium: Referring to *Yusufu s/o Lesso v R* (1952) 19 EACA 249, the Court of Appeal stated that 'That decision which differed from an earlier decision of this court in *R v Murume s/o Nayboba* (1945) 12 EACA 80 must no doubt be considered in relation to the facts of that case, and we should not be prepared to accept the proposition that no act of tresspass to property could ever amount to "a wrongful act or insult … done to … a person".'

A lawful act cannot constitute provocation

It is clear from Section 193 that conduct can only constitute provocation if it is unlawful. And under Section 193 (3), the law emphasises that a lawful act is not provocation to any person for an assault. Were the position to be different, the law would be contradicting itself.

Case law has recognised various forms of conduct as wrongful and capable of provoking an ordinary person into killing another. The most common examples are the finding of a spouse in an act of adultery; verbal insults; infringing on another person's right to property (thefts), performing an act of witchcraft; physical assaults.

Examples of provocations
Adultery as provocative behaviour
Where a person finds a spouse in circumstances which would lead a reasonable person to suspect that adultery had just been committed or was about to be committed, such a person may be able to plead provocation, if in the heat of passion she/he kills the spouse or the spouse's lover.

The question of provocation is ordinarily one of fact.

CASE: *R v Alayina* [1957] R & N 536 (Ny)
The accused went after dark in search of her reputed husband. She found him in a hut lying under a blanket with a young girl. The accused attacked the girl and wounded her with a knife. In the course of the struggle in the darkness of the hut, the girl's grandmother, who was also in the hut, was fatally stabbed.

Held: There was provocation to reduce murder to manslaughter.

CASE: *Chacha s/o Wamburu v R* [1953] 20 E.A.C.A 339
Accused came back at night. He went to his wife's house but she was not there. On going to his own house, he found his wife there. He asked her to build up the fire but instead she put it out with water. She then went out and got some grass and threw it at him and ran away. He suspected her, picked up his spear to search the house, and at that moment a man ran out of the house. The man tripped over some sticks outside and accused killed him with his spear.

Held: On appeal against a murder conviction, the Court of Appeal for Eastern Africa held *inter alia* that:

> The question whether a spouse is 'taken in the act of adultery' is essentially one of fact and need not be answered in accordance with the strict literal meaning of those words. It is not necessary that the wife and adulterer should be caught during the actual period of intercourse. If they are found together in circumstances from which immediately recent intercourse is, and can safely and correctly be inferred ... 'they are found in the act of adultery' ... For example, if they were undressed and in the same bed, they would clearly satisfy the rule.

Verbal insults can constitute provocation
Provocative conduct can be in the form of either an act or an insult.

CASE: *Rex v Hussein s/o Mohamed.* 9 EACA 52
The accused alleged that his father-in-law was planning to move to Nairobi and to take his daughter, the accused's wife, with him. Accused finally forbade his wife to go. She replied: 'Go away, *sala, budmash, harami*' (terms of abuse which literally mean 'brother-in-law, vagabond, scoundrel'). She spat at him and said 'I have seen many males like you and I shall see in the future. You are not the only man in the world; ... open the door for me, I want to go to my father just now. I do not want to live with you.'

Accused lost his self-control, seized a dagger and stabbed his wife many times and she died. The two assessors were of the opinion that if a wife utters those particular words to her husband, words so bad and with deep hidden meaning, the man would naturally lose the power to control himself.

Result: The East African Court of Appeal was in agreement with the assessors and returned a verdict of manslaughter based on provocation.

CASE: *Chacha s/o Wamburu v R* [1953] 20 EACA 339 (See above for details of the case)
In addition to the ruling on a definition of adultery, the Court of Appeal for Eastern Africa held *inter alia* that there is no rule that 'mere words' cannot be sufficient provocation to reduce an intentional killing to manslaughter. Infringing on another person's right to property, trespass and theft can constitute provocation

The defence of provocation in regard to property
This is not always successful, but depends on the facts of the individual case.
In *Mabonga v R* [1974] EA176, in a judgement read by Chief Justice Wambuzi the Court of Appeal for East Africa said:

> As regards the question of provocation, the defence submitted that the deceased's acts amounted to sufficient provocation to reduce the killing to manslaughter. Counsel for the crown drew our attention to the case of *Yusuf s/o Lesso v Republic* in which it was held that the definition of provocation is confined to wrongful acts done to the person and does not extend to wrongful acts done to property ... that decision, which differed from an earlier decision of this court in *R v Murume*, must no doubt be considered in relation to the facts of that case, and we should not be prepared to accept the proposition that no acts of trespass to property could ever amount to 'a wrongful act or insult ... done to ... a person' ... *Each case must be judged on its own facts.* [My emphasis]

And in *Marwa s/o Robi v R* [1959] EA 660 (East African Court of Appeal) the issue was not whether there had been provocation by a trespass but whether 'the means adopted by the appellant to resist the taking of the cattle were utterly out of proportion to the tort which was being committed'. (See p.2 for case details.)

CASE: *R v Murume s/o Nayboba* [1945]12 EACA 80 (Court of Appeal for Eastern Africa)
The accused had suffered thefts of his produce from time to time. He was aroused at night when he heard a noise of his sugarcane being pulled. In his words, the accused said: ' found someone in my shamba stealing from me. I killed him. I was very angry.'
    The court held that acts of trespass to property can amount to a wrongful act or insult done to a person i.e. provocation.
    In the words of the court, '... we should not be prepared to accept the proposition that no act of trespass to property could ever amount to 'a wrongful act or insult ... done to ... a person.'

CASE: *Yusufu s/o Lesso v Republic* (1952) 19 EACA 247 (Court of Appeal for Eastern Africa)
The appellant was woken at midnight by a noise as if someone was digging at the wall

at the back of his house. He seized a billhook and seeing two persons running away, pursued them. One of them fell down and the appellant struck him several times on the head with the billhook killing him.

Held: The question of provocation does not arise in the case of wrongful acts done to property.

CASE: *Uganda v Ssenabulya* [1978] HCB 27 (High Court) (Butagira)
The accused was charged with murder of the deceased persons. The two deceased persons met their death when they attempted to steal the accused's hen. Counsel for the accused raised the issue of provocation contending that the accused was provoked because his hen had been stolen.

Held *inter alia*:
Provocation must be confined to wrongful acts done to the person and does not extend to wrongful acts done to property. *Yusufu s/o Lesso v Republic* (1952) 19 EACA 247. For to extend the ambit of provocation would lead to wide scale legal licensing of killing of people. Thus in as far as provocation was related to the theft of the hen, in the instant case, it was not legal provocation.

Physical assaults as provocation

For physical assaults to be admitted as provocation, the reaction of the accused must be considered such that a 'normal' person would feel. If the court feels that the accused over-reacted the plea of provocation is likely to be rejected. On the other hand, in some cases, if the accused as been convincingly threatened with death, the plea may be admitted.

CASE: *Obong Richard s/o Ocen v Uganda* Criminal Appeal 4/82 (Court of Appeal for Uganda)
Accused was convicted of murder. He admitted killing the deceased but pleaded self-defence and provocation. In regard to the defence of provocation the trial judge ruled that even if the deceased had provoked the accused by hitting him, the assault by the deceased was negligible, and a normal person would not be so provoked as to club the assaulter so savagely as to render him instantly unable to speak and to kill him a few hours thereafter. the trial judge ruled that a normal person would not act that way and thus rejected the plea.

The Court of Appeal held that the trial judge's opinion was a misdirection of the law. It is not the law that a slight assault can never provoke the victim into mounting a more serious assault on the person offering the provocation.

Witchcraft as provocation

Several court cases show that witchcraft is a belief deeply embedded in Ugandan and indeed the East African society. Sometimes it is because of belief in witchcraft that homicides occur. Ugandan courts have taken judicial notice of this belief. Thus in *Republic v Juma* [1974] EA 336 the court noted *inter alia* that:

> Our people, whether we like it or not, have believed, are believing and will continue to

believe in witchcraft even if literacy were to become universal tomorrow morning. …
And judging from the very low level and slow pace of our technological advancement,
these beliefs shall remain with us for quite some time.

Under certain circumstances, an accused who kills another person whom he/she believes
to be practising witchcraft against him/her, is convicted of manslaughter rather than
murder, because witchcraft can be tantamount to provocative behaviour.

It is not only the courts that have taken note of the significance of witchcraft in
Ugandan society. Way back in 1957 the legislature passed a statute specifically dealing
with the subject – The Witchcraft Act, Chapter 124 of the Laws of Uganda. The Act
makes it an offence to practise witchcraft or to hold oneself out as a witch, to hire or
procure another person to practise witchcraft, or to consult with such practioner 'for
evil purposes'. (As Morris and Read (1966:302) said, 'this qualification reflects the
common distinction between the use of witchcraft for ill and the use of it for purposes
of divination or the cure of ill health'.)

Thus in *Uganda v Kevina Nanono* Criminal Revision No: MMU.2730 of 1973,
Chief Justice Wambuzi (as he was then) threw light on the offence created under the
Act. The accused was charged in two counts with threatening another with death by
means of witchcraft contrary to Section 3 (1) and being in possession of articles used
in witchcraft contrary to Sections 3 (1) and 5 respectively.

On revision it was held *inter alia* that: An offence is committed under this section
if a person directly or indirectly threatens another with death by witchcraft or by any
other supernatural means.

It is thus noted that witchcraft can constitute unlawful conduct and is thus capable
of being interpreted as legal provocation.

In view of the legislature's recognition of witchcraft as anti-social behaviour, it is
perhaps not surprising that judges appreciate the likelihood that anybody who perceives
him/herself to be in danger of its consequences would be partially justified to react
violently. The court's recognition of witchcraft as possible provocative behaviour is
also in line with the definition of provocation under Section 193 (3) of the Penal Code
Act that requires an act to be unlawful before it can be recognised as legally provocative.
(Section 193 (3): A lawful act is not provocation to any person for an assault).

In HCCSC No. 123/76 the court revealed in great detail circumstances under which
witchcraft can constitute provocation thus:

> If the facts proved to establish that the victim was performing in the actual presence of
> the accused some act which the accused did genuinely believe, and which an ordinary
> person of the community to which the accused belongs would genuinely believe, to be
> an act of witchcraft against him or another person under his immediate care (which act
> would be a criminal offence under the criminal law (Witchcraft) Ordinance of Uganda …
> he might be angered to such an extent as to be deprived of the power of self-control and
> induced to assault the person doing the act of witchcraft. And if this be the case, a
> defence of grave and sudden provocation is open to him. It must always be a question
> of fact as to whether he is in all the circumstances of the particular case acting in the heat
> of passion caused by grave and sudden provocation.

However, the court also noted that if the accused kills another person in revenge for supposedly causing a fatal bewitchment of a relative in the past, this would not be legal provocation. In other words, the killing must have been a result of an immediate act by the victim in the presence of the accused. As with other types of provocative behaviour, witchcraft must be immediate to the provocative behaviour.

Mere belief in witchcraft does not amount to legal provocation
An accused cannot plead provocation if he or she simply believes that witchcraft has been used. The belief must be supported by an immediate physical action by the deceased.

CASE: *Eria Galikuwa v R* (1951) 18 EACA 175 (Court of Appeal for Eastern Africa) The appellant had Shs 320 stolen from him and he got in touch with the deceased, who had a considerable reputation as a witchdoctor, in the hope that the deceased might recover the stolen money. On the first visit, the deceased asked the accused for various articles of property which he duly paid. On the second visit the deceased demanded more property and told the accused that unless he paid, the deceased's 'medicine would eat him up'.

The accused paid up. On the third visit, the deceased demanded Shs 1000 and again threatened that if the accused did not pay 'he would be eaten up.' The accused made attempts to look for the money but failed to get it. He then started hearing voices demanding payment or else he would die. As a result of the threats, the accused decided to kill the deceased 'to save his life'.

In cross-examination, the accused said inter alia 'when I heard the voice I was much frightened … no one would give the money. I decided to silence him. I felt quite normal. … if I did not raise the money I would be killed. I honestly thought that …'

The appellant was convicted before the High Court of Uganda of murder. He admitted that having been threatened with death unless he paid the witchdoctor Shs 1000 and, being unable to obtain this sum, he killed the deceased in order to save his own life.

Held on appeal:
1. The act causing death must prove to be done in the heat of passion, i.e. in anger; fear of immediate death is not sufficient.
2. If the facts establish that the deceased was performing some act in the presence of the accused which he believed, and an ordinary person of his community would genuinely believe, was an act of witchcraft against him and the accused was so angered as to be deprived of his self-control, the defence of grave and sudden provocation was open to the accused.
3. A belief in witchcraft *per se* did not constitute a circumstance of excuse or mitigation for killing a person believed to be a witch or wizard when there is no immediate provocative act. The provocative act must amount to a criminal offence under the criminal law.
4. The provocation must be not only grave but sudden and the killing have been done in the heat of passion.
5. The provocative act might indicate a future intention on the part of the doer

and might therefore be of such a nature as to come within the definition of legal provocation.

Judgement:

The court said *inter alia*:

> A mere belief founded on something metaphysical, as opposed to something physical, that a person is causing the death of another by supernatural means, however honest that belief, does not constitute in law a circumstance of excuse or mitigation for killing when there is no provocative act.

CASE: *Republic v Juma* [1974] E.A. 336

The deceased was a reputed wizard. He inspired fear in his son – the accused - by first asking him to train in witchcraft. According to the accused, his father roused him early one morning and took him to the bush. He then asked the accused to throw down the blanket with which he covered himself and to proceed naked so that he could take lessons in witchcraft. The accused was afraid and he declined to take any such training. The father was displeased with him. He therefore threatened to bewitch the accused. So great was the accused's fear that he ran off to Kiwere in order to escape from the diabolical influence of the deceased. But at Kiwere a snake wrapped itself on his leg and when he consulted a medicineman there, he was told that this misfortune was traceable to his father. When he returned home to his father, the deceased assured him that it would not serve him to run away. His magic would reach him wherever he chose to go. Thereafter relations between father and son grew worse. One day, as the accused was drinking at a pombe shop, his father came. The accused then, out of respect and generosity, bought him some beer. Instead of being grateful to him, the deceased became abusive and quarrelsome. The accused then moved off to some private place with his friend and continued drinking.

His stomach later on swelled so much that he passed out next day. His mother rushed for the cell-leader on whose intervention the deceased revived and cured his son. From then on the accused became convinced that his life was in danger. The threat the deceased had made to him that he would kill his son for despising him became a sword of Damocles to the accused. On· the fateful day the accused drank from morning till night. When he returned home that night, he made up his mind to get rid of the deceased before the deceased made good the threat to kill him. The accused entered the deceased's room, picked up an axe from the corner and hacked to death his father who was at the time sleeping and unsuspecting. He then pulled the body to the field close to the house and partly buried it.

Judgement by Kwikima Ag. J.:

> ... His belief in the potency of witchcraft, being purely metaphysical, cannot be verified either empirically, or by corroboration. It suffices to say that the accused or for that matter any member of the society in which the accused lived, would have felt exactly as the accused: that the deceased, a reputed and feared wizard and medicine man, would use witchcraft and magic to kill him. Such feeling would be intensified by the harrowing experience which the accused went through.

... That he killed his father is unquestionable. It is likewise unquestionable that the accused harboured, and in his view, he was justified to harbour a belief that the deceased was going to kill him with witchcraft. By his conduct and utterances, the deceased left his son in no doubt that he would at any time kill him. But as I have already pointed out, belief in witchcraft is metaphysical, and, as was pointed out in *R v Kajuna* [1945] 12 EACA 104:

'The mere belief founded on something physical, that a person is causing the death of another by supernatural means, however honest that belief, does not constitute in law a circumstance of excuse or mitigation for killing a person when there is no provocation.'

It should not be forgotten, however, that the cumulative effect of the threat and suffering of the accused must have been to enhance the mortal fear which the accused had for his life.

But this is not to say that the law as it stands at present would come to the rescue of the unfortunate majority in this country who firmly believe in witchcraft. The only conditions under which the killing of a wizard would mitigate the offence of murder have been set out thus:

'(1) The act causing death must be ... done in heat of passion ... fear of immediate death is not sufficient... The provocation must be not only grave but sudden and the killing must have been done in the heat of passion. (6) The provocative act may indicate a future intention on the part of the doer and might therefore be of such a nature as to come within the definition of legal provocation (*Eria Galikuwa* v R (1951) 18 E.A.C.A 175).'.

Had the deceased therefore killed his father on his return from Kiwele at the time when the deceased threatened to kill him for his disrespect, the accused would have been exonerated from murder ...

As the facts of this case stand, the accused cannot be said to have either been provoked or to have killed in the heat of passion. His act was cool, calculated and deliberate. It was no doubt prompted by the accused's belief in witchcraft and his intense fear for his life. It was, to the accused or to anyone in his station in life, either his death or that of his father. So he resolved to save himself by killing his father first. Unfortunately for him the law does not allow the killing of wizards like it does the killing of snakes and other prowling beasts.

Result: Accused guilty of murder.

CASE: *Rex v Peter Wabwire s/o Malemo* Criminal Appeal No.82/1949[5]
The appellant was convicted of the murder of his wife. The defence was that the appellant genuinely and reasonably believed that the deceased was practising witchcraft against him with the intention of killing him and that when he found her actually in possession of 'medicine' and she declined to say from where she had obtained it his belief was confirmed and he killed her.

Held:
1. That the evidence could not justify a finding that the deceased woman's conduct led the appellant to believe that she was presently and instantly intending to kill him.
2. That a belief in witchcraft *per se* will not constitute a circumstance of excuse

or mitigation when there is no provocative act, and that in order to succeed on a plea of legal provocation the facts proved must establish that the victim was performing in the actual presence of the accused some act which the accused did genuinely believe, and which an ordinary person of the community to which the accused person belongs would genuinely believe to be an act of witchcraft. *Fabiano Kinene*, 8 E.A.C.A 96 cited with approval.

3. That the definition of legal provocation ... as being a wrongful act or insult done by the person killed clearly means that the act or insult must be something of a physical nature which is visible or audible to the person to whom it is done. R v *Kajuna s/o Mbake*, 12 E.A.C.A 104 cited.

4. That there might upon occasion be a wrongful act indicative of a future intention on the part of the doer and which therefore might be of such a nature as to come within the definition of legal provocation as set out in the relevant section of the Penal Code.

CASE: *Salvatorio Ayoo, Joel Ogei v Uganda* Criminal Appeal No.27/85 (Supreme Court)

The two appellants were indicted together with eight others for the murder of Oruk. On the day before the death of the deceased, A1 went to the home of Achako where there was a drinking party and informed the people that there was going to be a meeting at the home of the deceased at 8 a.m. the following day. He told them that he had caught the deceased with herbs for killing people. The following day the people gathered at the house of the deceased at the appointed time. The deceased was not at home, he had gone to his garden. A1 and A2 were among the crowd. A1 and other people went to the deceased's garden to look for him. They brought him back with his hands tied at the back. He was then assaulted by sticks and stones by the crowd and he died on the spot.

One of the grounds of appeal was that the learned trial judge erred in law in rejecting the defence of provocation due to the fact that the deceased practised witchcraft.

Held: It was held by the Supreme Court that mere suspicion will not avail in a case of witchcraft. In the present case there was no wrongful act or insult on the part of the deceased done or offered to an ordinary person in order to provoke the appellants, it was mere suspicion that the man practised witchcraft.

Belief coupled with other circumstances may constitute provocation

Courts emphasise that it is not a belief in witchcraft *per se* that constitutes mitigation for killing the person believed to be a witch. The belief must be accompanied by an immediate provocative act of the witch.

CASE: *Kenjeru w/o Karindori* HCCSC No.215/91

The deceased and the accused were co-wives. The deceased entered the accused's bedroom and removed the latter's blanket and spread it on her own bed. The accused tried to retrieve her blanket but the deceased resisted those attempts. The accused got a hoe and pursued the deceased and cut her across the skull once. The victim died immediately. The defence counsel for the accused argued that the fatal attack was provoked by the belief that the victim intended to bewitch the accused and her child. He submitted that the deceased's action angered the accused, it was a threat of bewitchment and the accused had decided to finish off the deceased before she could harm her.

The defence counsel further argued that the fact that the accused had lost four children earlier on and believed that those deaths were a result of witchcraft, this should be taken into consideration. Furthermore, it was argued that since the accused's only surviving child was sick at the time of the assault, the accused's fear that the deceased aim was to finish off that child as well, was understandable.

Held: That the accused had killed on provocation and was thus guilty of manslaughter and not murder.

CASE: *Uganda v Ntusi and Another* [1977] HCB 64 (High Court)

The accused was indicted for murder. In his statement the accused said that the deceased (D) had killed the accused's brother (A) by witchcraft. Before his brother's death, the accused had entreated D not to kill A but the deceased had refused and the brother died when he was mad. Then after sometime, D bewitched the accused's mother who became sick.

While the accused was working in his garden the deceased (D) passed by. The accused then pleaded with him that his mother should not die as was the case with his elder brother. D then told the accused that he, too, would die before he even buried his mother. The accused got angry and cut the deceased with a panga on the head. The accused then went and reported himself to the authorities.

Issue: Whether the defence of provocation was available.

Held:
1. It is no defence for one to kill another on suspicion that the other has bewitched him or his dear one. However there are circumstances where belief in witchcraft coupled with other circumstances may furnish legal provocation.
2. In the instant case legal provocation was established because the threat of death by the deceased considered in the light of the fact that the accused had lost his brother whom he believed honestly to have been bewitched by the deceased, and the fact that his mother was awaiting the same fate, constituted a wrongful act of such a nature which deprived him of self control and made him to react the way he did in heat of passion.

Result: Acquitted of murder, convicted of manslaughter.

CASE: *Uganda v Nambwegere s/o Rovumba* ULR [1972] 15

The accused was indicted on a charge of murder contrary to Section 183 (now 188) of the Penal Code Act. The accused admitted killing the deceased but set up defences of provocation and self-defence, against a background of alleged witchcraft. The deceased was a well known and feared witchdoctor, and it was strongly suspected that he had been responsible for the death of accused's wife. On the day the deceased met his death, he was seen walking with the accused in a friendly manner. The accused was carrying a panga. Shortly afterwards a witness heard some noise and saw the deceased lying on the ground with serious injuries on the head and neck. The accused was standing near the deceased with a panga. Accused admitted killing the deceased because the deceased had bewitched his wife.

In defence the accused claimed that while walking with the deceased on a path, the deceased boasted to him that he had killed his wife because she had refused his advances to befriend her. Deceased added that he would kill the accused and his children as well. Accused tried to walk past the deceased but the deceased seized the piece of cloth he was wearing round his neck. Deceased also tried to take away the accused's panga and he thought deceased would kill him.

Held: As the accused believed that the deceased had supernatural powers and this belief was shared by most people in the village, he honestly (but obviously mistakenly) suspected that the deceased had caused his wife's death. The deceased's sudden boast confirmed his worst suspicions and to this was added a threat that he and his children would meet the same fate. Further the deceased had seized the accused's piece of cloth and pulled it tight round his neck while at the same time trying to disarm the accused of his panga. Judging the accused by the standard of a reasonable member of the unsophisticated community to which he belonged, legal provocation had been made out sufficiently to reduce the killing to manslaughter.

Also held that there is no rule that an intention to kill deprives the accused of a defence of provocation.

Result: Guilty of manslaughter.

Note: The judge did not specify what particular wrongful act was offered by the deceased to the accused to induce him to retaliate. Was it the threat that he would soon be killed by the deceased or the pulling of the accused's loose cloth round his neck?

CASE: *Uganda v Bonefasi Muvuga* ULR [1973] 30
The accused was indicted for the murder of Regina. The accused had lost a child, and as the mother of the child was away, he invited the deceased to stay with him and the dead child on the night of the death. The deceased accepted the invitation. The accused noticed that the deceased was not upset by the death of his child and he believed she had killed the child by witchcraft. The following day after the funeral, the accused went to drink at a nearby bar. When he returned and got into his house, he noticed somebody squatting in the doorway of his bedroom, facing into the room. When he asked the person who it was and what she was doing, the deceased ran into the courtyard, holding a piece of cloth which she threw away into the grass.

Having recognised the 'stranger' as the deceased, the accused inquired why she had been squatting as a witch, and suggested that she may have killed his child by witchcraft. Thereupon the deceased replied 'If I have bewitched your child go and accuse me to the authorities. If you are not careful I will also kill you.' The accused then attacked the deceased with a panga, inflicted multiple injuries on her which caused instant death.

Held: The threat by the deceased to kill the accused as she had killed his child and the fact that the deceased had been found in the accused's house in suspicious circumstances and that the deceased was holding something which she chose to hide from the accused, amounted to legal provocation.

Result: Guilty of manslaughter.

Judgement: Justice Manyindo *inter alia* said:

> In *Yovan v Uganda* [1970] E.A. 405 Duffus P said that … 'In considering this case the trial judge relied on the principles relating to provocation as explained by this court in *Eria Galikuwa* and having held that the substantive act of provocation here was a threat to cause appellant's death, said, following that decision that "a mere threat to cause death cannot be considered as a physical provocative act".' With respect we are of the view that the decision in Galikuwa should not be regarded as laying down a general rule but must be interpreted with reference to the facts of that case. There may be cases where a threat to kill taken with other existing circumstances could amount to legal provocation.

> Applying the above principle to the present case, I am satisfied that the threat by the deceased to kill the accused as she had killed his child, plus the fact that the deceased had been found in the accused's house in suspicious circumstances and that the deceased was holding something which she chose to hide from the accused, amounted to legal provocation.

CASE: *Yovan v Uganda* [1970] EA 405 (Court of Appeal for East Africa)
Two of the appellant's children suddenly died. The appellant suspected that the deceased, an elderly woman and his stepmother, had killed the two children either by witchcraft or poison. On the same day, the appellant went to the old woman's house and blamed her for the deaths. The deceased did not deny the allegation but said to the appellant that he would also die before he could perform the funeral ceremony for his two children. The appellant said he got annoyed at this stage and cut the deceased on her head and then she fell into her fireplace. The deceased's hut caught fire and was completely burnt with the deceased inside. The deceased died from the injury to her head and from extensive burns both inflicted or caused by the appellant, either of which injuries would in any event have caused her death.

Held *inter alia* that:
1. A threat to cause death of the accused may amount to provocation, depending on the circumstances.
2. … the act of the deceased in threatening to cause death of the appellant, presumably by witchcraft, must be viewed not in isolation but in the context of the appellant's children having just died, the appellant honestly believing the deceased to have been responsible for their deaths, and the deceased knowing this belief. We are unable to say that the uttering of such threats by the deceased, in these circumstances, could never constitute a wrongful act and thus legal provocation.

1. I presume the court meant that it is not every wrongful act that will be considered as legal provocation, as capable of making an ordinary person lose self control.
2. Also cited in *Uganda v Peter Ogwang* Crim Session No. 306 of 1992; High Court.
3. http:Canada.justice.gc.ca/en/cons/rccd/sectionlpl.html. Page 3. Accessed on 5/05/04.
4. http://canada.justice.gc.ca/en/cons/rccd/sectionlpl.html page 3. Accessed on 5/5/04.
5. Appeal from decision of High Court of Uganda.

9
Self-defence and murder

Although the defence of self-defence is a general defence and is not limited/specific to murder, it is important to discuss here its applicability to murder, because it is a defence commonly pleaded on murder charges, often together with provocation. Indeed as pointed out by the Court of Appeal for Uganda in *Didasi Kebengi v Uganda* [1978] HCB 216:

> ... in almost all cases, the element of self-defence may and does often merge into the element of provocation.

Under Section 17 of the Uganda Penal Code, it is provided that 'criminal responsibility for the use of force in the defence of person and property shall be determined according to the principles of English law.' Consequently, self-defence is basically a question of judge made or case law.

A successful plea of self-defence leads to an acquittal: self-defence is a complete defence.

In *Ojepan Ignatius v Uganda* Criminal Appeal 25/1995 (Supreme Court of Uganda), the court dealt with the law of self defence and stated: 'It is based on common sense that a man who is attacked may defend himself. It is both good law and good sense that he may do, but may only do what is reasonably necessary. But everything will depend on the particular facts and circumstances. As it was observed by the Privy Council in *Palmer v R* (1971), All ER 1077 at 1088:

> It may in some cases be only sensible and clearly possible to take some simple avoiding action. Some attacks may be serious and dangerous. Others may not be. If there is some relatively minor attack it would not be common sense to permit some action of retaliation which was wholly out of proportion to the necessities of the situation. If an attack is serious so that it puts someone in immediate peril then immediate defensive action may be necessary. If the moment is one of surprise for someone in imminent danger he may have to avert the danger by some instant reaction ... If there has been attack so that defence is reasonably necessary it will be recognised that a person defending himself cannot weigh to a nicety the exact measure of his necessary defensive action.

Where evidence reveals a possibility that the accused killed in self-defence, the onus is on the prosecution to prove the guilt of the accused beyond reasonable doubt.

In *Selemani v Republic* [1963] E.A 442 (Court of Appeal for Eastern Africa) It was stated that:

> ... If a person against whom a forcible and violent felony is being attempted repels force by force and in so doing kills the attacker the killing is justifiable, provided there was a reasonable necessity for the killing or an honest belief based on reasonable grounds that it was necessary and the violence attempted by or reasonably apprehended from the attacker is really serious. It would appear that in such a case there is no duty in law to retreat, though no doubt questions of opportunity of avoidance of disengagement would be relevant to the question of reasonable necessity for the killing. In other cases of self-defence where no violent felony is attempted a person is entitled to use reasonable

force against an assault, and if he is reasonably in apprehension of serious injury, provided he does all that he is able in the circumstances, by retreat or otherwise to break off the fight or avoid the assault, he may use such force, including deadly force, as is reasonable in the circumstances. In either case if the force used is excessive, but if the other elements of self-defence are present there may be a conviction of manslaughter.

In *George Kanalusasi v Uganda,* Criminal Appeal No.10/1988, the Supreme Court quashed a conviction of murder against the accused and substituted a conviction of manslaughter under Section 182, on the basis that whereas the accused was entitled to strike the intruder, the force he used in striking an unarmed person was excessive.

In *Uganda v Sebastiano Otti* [1994-95] HCB 21. High Court, it was held, *inter alia*, that 'death is excusable when caused in self defence. To constitute self defence there must have been an unlawful attack on the accused who as result reasonably believed that he was in imminent danger of death or serious bodily harm and it was necessary for him to use force to repel the attack made upon him. Also the force used by the accused must have been reasonably necessary to prevent the threatened danger.

The use of excessive force in self defence renders the offence manslaughter see e.g *Kabengi v Uganda* [1978] HCB 216 (Court of Appeal for Uganda).

CASE: *Uganda v Ojok* [1992-1993] HCB 54
The accused was indicted for murder. On the relevant date, the deceased went to UCB Panyimur Branch where the accused was on guard duty. The accused ordered the deceased to stop and fired a shot. The deceased started running away and the accused pursued him. The accused fired a second shot a distance from the bank. Minutes later the accused fired the fatal shot about 100 metres away from the bank. He then reported to the police that he had killed a person. He pleaded self-defence.

Held *inter alia*:
1. The law on self-defence consists of four elements:
   - That there must be an attack on the accused.
   - The accused must as a result have believed on reasonable ground that he was in imminent danger of death or serious bodily harm.
   - The accused must have believed it necessary to use force to repel the attack made upon him.
   - The force used by the accused must be such force as the accused believed on reasonable grounds to have been necessary to prevent or resist the attack. In determining whether the extent of the force used by the accused was reasonably necessary regard must be had to all the circumstances of the case.
2. It is trite law that a person attacked in such circumstances that he reasonably believes his life to be in imminent danger is entitled to use force, even deadly force, to repel the attack and the decision whether the accused is placed in such situation as necessitates the use of force to protect his life is one of fact and depends on the circumstances of each case. However it is the law that the accused would not be availed the defence of self-defence if there are no

reasonable grounds upon which he based his belief that the force used w. s reasonably necessary to repel the attack.

3. Although the law is that a person attacked may use such force as he reasonably believes is necessary to prevent or resist the attack or such force as he, in the circumstances, reasonably believes to be necessary for his protection, he must evince a willingness to temporise or disengage and perhaps to make some physical withdrawal and if the opportunity to avoid conflict exists but instead of doing so, force is resorted to, this may be used to determine whether the force used was reasonably necessary in the circumstances. Where, however, a person is faced with an unexpected, violent and felonious attack, he is not, in defending himself, expected to weigh to a nicety the exact measure of his necessary defensive action, since it is known that fear, pain and surprise can physiologically so change a person as to literally take him out of his normal self. However, if the attack is relatively minor, the law cannot look with leniency at retaliation which is wholly out of proportion to the necessity of the occasion.

CASE: *Uganda v Yowana Kalungi* Criminal Session Case No. 97/1974 (Before Justice Saied)

The accused was indicted for the murder of one Andrea. The accused admitted killing the deceased to a number of witnesses and put up a defence of self-defence. He claimed that the deceased attacked first and, in self-defence, he cut the deceased with a panga. The post mortem report revealed a cut wound on the right side of the deceased's forehead, 7in x 4in deep, going vertically up towards the top of the head fracturing the frontal bone. Another cut wound was found on the right temporal region 4in x 2in deep which was horizontal, fracturing the right temporal bone.

Held:

1. Applying *R v Julien* [1969] 2 All ER 856, it was not necessary for the accused to retreat in face of an attack by the deceased so long as he tried to make some 'physical withdrawal'.

2. Applying *Mhabi s/o Ntungi v Rep* EACA (1972), it was not an essential element of self-defence for the retaliation to be proportionate. The reactions of a man who was attacked and sought to defend himself should not be too nicely judged.

Result: Accused acquitted.

Cases cited with approval:

1. *Alfred Tajar v Uganda* (EACA) Crim App Rep 167/69
2. *R v Julien* [1969] 2 All ER 856
3. *R v Palmer* [1971] All ER. 1077
4. *Mhabi s/o Ntungi v Republic* (EACA) Crim. App Rep 141/72
5. *Serwadda v Uganda* (EACA) Crim App Rep 142/73

CASE: *Obong Richard s/o Ocen v Uganda*, Criminal Appeal 4/82 (Supreme Court of Uganda)

The appellant admitted killing the deceased but pleaded self-defence and provocation. He claimed that while at the house of Atang, he had asked the deceased to settle a pending debt owed to him. That the deceased refused to pay up and a quarrel ensued. That the deceased hit the accused twice with a pestle. That the appellant disarmed the deceased and beat him on the head with the same pestle, 'in self-defence'.

The trial judge rejected the accused's evidence and believed the prosecution case to the effect that the accused had hit the deceased without any provocation or attack from the deceased.

The appellant was convicted of murder and sentenced to death. He appealed against conviction and sentence.

Held on appeal: On self-defence, the Supreme Court agreed with the trial judge and held *inter alia* that the defence of self-defence would not avail the appellant as he was clearly not in any danger when he struck the deceased fatally as he had already disarmed him.

In their judgement, the Justices of Appeal said:

> Once the appellant had disarmed the deceased he could not in law hit him back in self-defence since he was no longer in fear of immediate danger. However, we cannot agree with the trial judge that once one is attacked one must always run away as fast and as far as he can. The law on this point is seems clear. It is that if one is attacked violently, one may repel the attack with force and may even kill the attacker if his life is in grave danger or if he honestly believes that it is in such danger. If he had a chance to disengage he should do so without resort to the use of force against his attacker. See *Manzi Mengi v R* (1964) E.A.C.A 289.

A plea of self-defence in defence of property

Defending one's property – whether household or animal – raises the issue of self-defence.

In *Kasto Budebo v Uganda*, Criminal Appeal No 22/1993 (Supreme Court), it was held:

1. A householder is entitled either to seek to arrest or to expel an intruder. He does not have to retreat, but he may use reasonable force to effect his purpose.
2. In many cases, no hard and fast line can be drawn between self defence and defence of property. (E.g where an intruder enters someone's dwelling)
3. Where he uses unnecessary force in self-defence or defence of property, he will be guilty of manslaughter.

CASE: In *Marwa s/o Robi v R* [1959] EA 660, East African Court of Appeal

The appellant was convicted of murder for spearing to death the deceased after a dispute over cattle which the deceased claimed and had gone to the appellant to collect. On appeal it was assumed in the appellant's favour that the deceased had gone to reclaim cattle to which he had no legitimate claim and that the deceased actually attempted to drive away the cattle. The trial judge had found that no force was used against the appellant, although the deceased had carried a stick when he went towards the appellant's boma. On appeal, it was argued for the appellant inter alia that the trial judge misdirected himself as to the law applicable to cases of homicide in defence of property and that he had erred in finding that there was no sufficient provocation to reduce the offence to manslaughter. (See also pages 2, 9, 102 and 104)

Issue: Whether killing in defence of property justified under Section 17 (now 15) of the Penal Code Act.

Held *inter alia*:
1. It must be a question of fact in each case whether the degree of force used in defence of property which caused death was, in the particular circumstances of the case, justifiable, or, if not justifiable, whether it was such as to amount only to manslaughter,or was so excessive as to constitute the offence of murder.
2. In driving off the cattle the deceased was no doubt committing a tresspass, but the means adopted by the appellant to resist the taking of the cattle were utterly out of proportion to the tort which was being committed.

At page 663, the court said:

> The appellant was no doubt entitled to use reasonable force to prevent taking of the cattle, and if, in good faith, he had used more force than was reasonable and had thereby killed … no doubt the offence would only have amounted to manslaughter …

CASE: *Uganda v Fabiano Mukama* Criminal Session Case 161/1972 (High Court)
The accused was indicted for murder. On the material evening, the accused was informed by a neighbour that someone had entered his house. The accused rushed home and on arrival in his house, the deceased ran and collided with him in the dark. Both men fell down. The accused got up, picked a hatchet from nearby and hit the deceased on the head and leg. The deceased died instantly of a crushed skull.
He pleaded that he acted in self-defence and defence of property.

Held *inter alia*:
1. The accused, like any other person, was expected to guard his property against thieves using no more force than was necessary in the circumstances.
2. The accused was entitled to defend his own life against the deceased by administering the three blows as he thought his life was in danger. In such a heated moment as that, it was difficult to judge what force was necessary to overcome the attacker. The test was for one to place himself in the shoes of the accused in question and consider what he would have done in the circumstances.
3. The court would find that the accused's action was justifiable.

Result: Accused found not guilty and acquitted.

CASE: *Manzi Mengi v R* [1964] EA 289 (Court of Appeal for Eastern Africa)
The appellant found cattle on his shamba being tended by two children who said that

the deceased had told them to bring the cattle there. The appellant drove away the cattle and went to fetch a panga to mend his fence. On his return he found the cattle there again and the children told him that they had brought the cattle back on the deceased's instructions. The appellant again drove the cattle away. While he was repairing the fence the deceased appeared armed with a bow and arrows and after abusing the appellant threatened to kill him. He then fired an arrow at the appellant but missed. The appellant then told the deceased not to kill him and the deceased replied 'I am going to kill you.' The deceased then crossed the fence and entered the shamba and struck the appellant twice with the bow and tried to stab the appellant with arrows whereupon the appellant struck the deceased repeatedly with the panga as a result of which the deceased died.

When charged with murder, the defence of the appellant was that he had acted in self-defence to save his life. The trial judge found that the appellant stood in danger of his life, that if he had not made use of the panga, the deceased would probably have killed him and that the appellant had acted in self-defence but had used excessive force. The judge accordingly convicted the appellant of manslaughter.

Held:

1. The onus was on the prosecution to show that the appellant was not acting in self-defence; it was for the prosecution to show that there was time before the fatal blow was struck for the appellant to have realised that he was out of danger and desisted; this onus was not discharged;
2. The appellant was entitled to use lethal force, and what he did, after he had used it, could not affect his liability on the charge of murder.

In the judgement the court noted that:

> if ever there was a case in which the victim of an attack was justified in using violence, including lethal violence, this is such a case. It seems the trial judge had in mind the number of blows struck; he may have been of the opinion that the retaliation by the appellant continued after the need was past. The onus is on the prosecution to show that the appellant was not acting in self defence. It is therefore upon the prosecution to show that there was a time before a fatal blow was struck that the appellant should have realised he was out of danger and desisted.

Result: Appeal allowed. Conviction and sentence quashed.

CASE: *Yoweri Damulira v R*, Criminal Appeal No.48/1956 (Court of Appeal for Eastern Africa)

On the relevant night, the accused was sleeping in his house. The house was made of mud and thatch. At the back of the house and forming part of it was a chicken roost. The back wall of the house was one of the walls of the chicken roost and there was an entrance into the house from the chicken roost. Late in the night, he was awakened by hearing the door of the chicken roost being opened. He called out twice but received no answer. He heard the door being opened again and he went outside. Behind a tree about 4 feet from the house he saw a 'bulky thing'. He struck the intruder three times.

Although the accused said he thought he was striking at an animal, the trial judge was satisfied that the accused knew he was striking a person, a thief. The accused was convicted of murder.

Issues: One of the issues on appeal was whether the appellant was justified in using the degree of force he did in defence of property.

Held on appeal: The appellant was entitled to drive off a person who was attempting to break into his house and, if necessary, to inflict death in doing so. As it is stated in Archbold's *Criminal Pleading Evidence and Practice*, 33rd ed p. 943 'If any person … attempts burglariously to break into a dwelling house in the night, and is killed in the attempt, the slayer is entitled to acquittal for the homicide is justifiable, and the killing is without felony.' But the homicide can be justified only if it is necessary. In *Russell on Crime*, 10th ed at 498 it is said 'It has been observed that as homicide committed in the prevention of forcible and atrocious crimes is justifiable only on the plea of necessity, it cannot be justified unless the necessity continues up to the time when the party is killed.'

At the time when the deceased was attacked by the appellant he had desisted, at least temporarily, from the attempt to break into the house and it was not at that time necessary for the appellant to use extreme force to prevent the deceased from breaking in. Had the appellant attacked the deceased when he was actually attempting to break into the house he would no doubt have been justified in using force as he did. He was, however, entitled to use such force as was reasonably necessary to expel the deceased from his premises or to arrest him, but the force he used was unnecessary and excessive in the circumstances.

Result: Murder set aside and manslaughter under Section 182 (now 187) substituted.

CASE: *Zedekia Lukwago v R* Criminal Appeal No.535/1955
On 4th June 1955, Yakobo's dead body was found in the accused's house. It bore six very severe wounds. Accused admitted that he inflicted the wounds and thereby killed the deceased. He pleaded self-defence and alleged that on the evening of the relevant date, he fastened both doors of his house and went to bed. He was awakened by the deceased pulling off his bedclothes and, on trying to capture the intruder, he was set upon. His violence against the intruder was in self-defence.

The trial judge *inter alia* held that the accused had used excessive force and that 'One must use all means to escape. In this case there was nothing to prevent the accused from running out of the back door … It is clear that according to the accused the deceased was trying to escape and all he needed to have done was to allow him escape.'

Held: On appeal against conviction, the Court of Appeal for Eastern Africa said *inter alia* that:

> It is not the law that a householder attacked in his own house by an intruder is required to use all means to escape. It is a mistake in such circumstances to draw a hard and fast distinction between the right of defence of property and the right of defence of the person. The householder is entitled either to seek to arrest or to expel

the intruder and, should he be attacked in so doing, to use all necessary force to repel such attack and to effect the arrest or the expulsion.

The defence of lawful arrest in protection of property

CASE: *Muhidini s/o Asuman v R* [1962] EA 383 (East African Court of Appeal)
The appellant was convicted of the murder of a youth. The deceased together with another youth entered a maize shamba after dark to steal produce. The alarm was raised, the appellant left his house with a panga and went to investigate. He encountered the deceased running away and slashed him as he ran past him. The blow cut the deceased on the thigh and killed him almost instantly. There was evidence that maize thefts were rampant in the area and that they were often by armed gangs. The trial judge convicted the accused of murder.

On appeal it was argued for the appellant that in the circumstances of the case, it could not be said that the force used was unreasonable, and that the appellant was entitled to acquittal.

In its judgement, the court referred to Section 32 and Section 19 of the Criminal Procedure Code of Tanganyika (equivalent to Section 15 and Section 2 of Uganda's Criminal Procedure Code Act)[1] which read as follows:

- Section 32 (1) Any private person may arrest any person who in his view commits a cognizable offence, or whom he reasonably suspects of having committed a felony.

- Section 19 (1) In making an arrest the police officer or other person making the same shall actually touch or confine the body of the person to be arrested, unless there be a submission to the custody by word or action.

- (2) If such person forcibly resists the endeavour to arrest him, or attempts to evade arrest, such police officer or other person may use all means necessary to effect the arrest.

Reference was also made to Section 19 of the Penal Code of Tanganyika (the equivalent of Uganda's current Section 16 of the Penal Code Act) which reads as follows:

Where any person is charged with a criminal offence arising out of the arrest, or attempted arrest, by him or her of a person who forcibly resists the arrest, or attempts to evade being arrested, the court shall, in considering whether the means used were necessary, or the degree of force used was reasonable, for the apprehension of that person, have regard to the gravity of the offence which had been or was being committed by such person and the circumstances in which the offence had been or was being committed by the person.

Having conceded that the appellant killed the deceased in the process of apprehension, it stated that the issue was whether the degree of force used was reasonable, taking into account the gravity of the offence.

The court stated that it is a question of fact in each case, whether the degree of force used in effecting an arrest is justifiable, or, if not justifiable, whether it was such as to amount only to manslaughter or was so excessive as to constitute the offence of murder.

Burden of proof in self-defence

CASE: *Uganda v No.UD 1131 Sgt. Kelly Omuge alias Rashid alias Tito Lumumba and Baduru Walakira Nyanzi.* Crim Session Case 95/1985 (High Court) The High Court cited *Chan Kan v Reg* (1955) 2 W.L.R. 192 with approval and said:

> In cases where the evidence discloses a possible defence of self-defence the onus remains throughout upon the prosecution to establish that the accused is guilty of murder and the onus is never upon the accused to establish his defence any more than it is for him to establish provocation or any other defence apart from that of insanity which is strictly not a defence.

---

1. Chapter 116 *Laws of Uganda*, Revised Edition, 2000.

10

Homicides related to Infants and unborn Children

Infanticide
Section 213 Penal Code Act[1]
Under Section 213 of the Uganda Penal Code Act, a woman who willfully causes the death of her own child will be treated as if she were guilty of manslaughter if the killing occurs under the following circumstances:
1. The child killed (the victim) must be the woman's biological child.
2. The child must be under the age of 12 months at the time of the homicide.
3. At the time of killing the woman's mind must have been disturbed.
4. The disturbance must have been by reason of her not having fully recovered from giving birth to the child or from the effect of lactation consequent upon the birth of the child.

Infanticide was originally created by the English Infanticide Act of 1922. Its obvious purpose was to mitigate the rigours of murder, especially at a time in England where the death penalty was mandatory for murder convictions.

Infanticide is a type of voluntary homicide since the law refers to it as willful causation of death. Since willful means *intentional* or *deliberate*, this implies that the woman in question will have had malice aforethought. The offence would have been murder, but for the creation of Section 213.

The law takes into account the circumstances under which the killing was done, and treats the offender more leniently than it does for murder. The offender is treated as if she were guilty of manslaughter. The appropriate section for sentencing is thus Section 190 which provides that:

> Any person who commits the felony of manslaughter is liable for imprisonment for life.

Infanticide is a sex-specific crime in that it can only be committed by women. Infanticide is evidence that the criminal law recognises post-natal depression. A woman pleads mental disturbance of such a nature as would not amount to insanity under the rule in McNaughten's case.

Infanticide can be looked at as a defence as well as an offence. The prosecution can prosecute a woman who has killed her child, under Section 213. On the other hand, a woman who is indicted for the murder of her own child who has not attained 12 months can plead infanticide, i.e that at the time of the killing, her mind was disturbed as a result of child delivery and the effect of lactation.

Burden of proof in infanticide
The evidential burden on the issue of disturbance of mind falls on the accused. That is, the mother who raises the defence must adduce evidence sufficient to raise the defence but just on a balance of probabilities. Where there is some evidence of mental disturbance, the onus is on the prosecution to disprove it, if a woman is to be convicted of murder.

In this, infanticide differs from diminished responsibility and insanity where the burden of proof is on the accused.

Strictly interpreted, infanticide is limited to the conditions laid down in the Section and the fact the deceased child was less than 12 months old is not sufficient to enable a woman successfully plead the defence. There must in addition be evidence that the balance of her mind was disturbed.[2]

Cases and rulings on infanticide
Soanes [1948] 1 All ER 289, CCA:
The fact that the deceased child was less than 12 months old was not sufficient to bring a woman under the ambit of infanticide. There had also to be evidence that the balance of the mother's mind was disturbed for one of the stated reasons.

Namayanja v R 20 EACA 204:
The Court of Appeal for Eastern Africa expressed the view that in cases of infanticide the standard of proof required to show a disturbance of the balance of the mind is not as high as in the case of a defence resting on insanity.

In relation to the pronouncements in *Namayanja*, Collingwood (1976:188) said:

> This may mean no more than that the accused has the evidential burden of adducing some evidence in support of a finding of infanticide. [3]

The Law of abortion
Abortion deals with foetuses which, if procured from the womb, would not be capable of living. Article 22 (2) of the 1995 Constitution provides that:

No person has the right to terminate the life of an unborn child except as may be authorised by law.

The effect of the provision is that abortion is prohibited. However, the provision creates exceptions to the general rule – there are circumstances in which the law may authorise termination of the life of an unborn child.

Uganda's legislature has not come up with any statute outlining circumstances under which abortion is authorised. However, the Uganda Penal Code criminalises conduct related to termination of the life of an unborn child.

Under Sections 141[4], 137[5] and 138[6] of the Penal Code, various parties are liable to punishment for engaging in conduct which may lead to abortion.

Under Section 141, any person who unlawfully engages in conduct geared towards procuring the miscarriage of a woman, is guilty of an offence.

The conduct may be in the form of administering poison to the woman or causing her to take any substance which is capable of leading to an abortion. It may also be the use of force of any kind with the intention that a miscarriage occurs.

Under this provision, it is irrelevant whether the woman was or was not pregnant at the time of the unlawful actions.

The offender is liable to imprisonment for 14 years.

Section 142 deals with a woman who with an intention of procuring her miscarriage, unlawfully, either administers a substance to herself or uses force of any kind or allows another person to administer such substance to her or to use force on her, for purposes of procuring an abortion.

To be caught by the law, the woman must indeed have been pregnant.

The offender is liable to imprisonment for 7 years.

Under Section 143 it is a crime to supply to or procure for any person, any material, knowing that it is going to be unlawfully used to procure the miscarriage of a woman.

Can procuration of a miscarriage be lawful?

It is noted that under the above sections, the word 'unlawfully' is used. This then raises the question, are there circumstances when procuration of a miscarriage is lawful? Are there circumstances in which the law authorises the termination of the life of an unborn child?

Section 224 of the Penal Code Act provides that:

> A person is not criminally responsible for performing in good faith and with reasonable care and skill a surgical operation ... upon an unborn child for the preservation of the mother's life, if the performance of the operation is reasonable, having regard to the patient's state at the time, and to all the circumstances of the case.

The effect of Section 224 is that if the life of the unborn child is terminated, in order to save the life of the woman, such procuration of miscarriage is not a crime.

The question, however, is what constitutes preservation of the mother's 'life'?

CASE In *Bourne* [1939] 1KB 687, *McNaughten* gave a wide meaning to the phrase 'for the purpose only of preserving the life of the mother'.

Facts: A young girl, not quite 15 years of age, was pregnant as the result of rape. A surgeon, of the highest skill, openly, in one of the London hospitals, without fee performed the operation of abortion. He was charged with unlawfully procuring the abortion.

Held: On a charge of procuring abortion, it is for the prosecution to prove beyond reasonable doubt that the operation was not performed in good faith for the purpose only of preserving the life of the mother. The surgeon did not have to wait until the patient was in peril of immediate death, but it was his duty to perform the operation if, on reasonable grounds and with adequate knowledge, he was of the opinion that the probable consequence of the pregnancy would be to make the patient a physical and mental wreck.

Note: The judge carefully distinguished between the act of the professional abortionist and an operation openly performed by a qualified surgeon.

He held that where the operation is performed by a person of no skill, with no medical qualifications, such a person would be guilty of unlawfully procuring an abortion.

Judgement

> The words 'for the preservation of the life of the mother' do not mean merely for the preservation of the life of the mother from instant death. There are cases where it is

reasonably certain that a woman will not be able to deliver the child with which she is pregnant. In such a case, where the doctor expects, basing his opinion upon the experience and knowledge of the profession, that the child cannot be delivered without the death of the mother, in those circumstances the doctor is entitled – and, indeed, it is his duty – to perform this operation with a view to saving the life of the mother, and in such a case it is obvious that the sooner the operation is performed the better. The law is *not* that the doctor has got to wait until the unfortunate woman is in peril of immediate death and then at the last moment snatch her from the jaws of death. He is not only entitled, but it is his duty, to perform the operation with a view to saving her life.

There are some who hold the view that the fact that the woman desires the operation to be performed is a sufficient justification for it. That is not the law. The desire of a woman to be relieved of her pregnancy is no justification for performing the operation.

On the other hand, there are people who, from what are said to be religious reasons, object to the operation being performed at all, in any circumstances. This is *not* the law either.

If a case arose where the life of the woman could be saved by performing the operation and the doctor refused to perform it because of some religious opinion, and the woman died, he would be in grave peril of being prosecuted on a charge of manslaughter by negligence. He would have no better defence than would a person who for some religious reason, refused to call in a doctor to attend his child, where a doctor could have been called in and the life of the child saved. If the father, for a religious reason refused to call in a doctor, he would be answerable to the criminal law for the death of his child.

The words 'for the purpose of preserving the life of the mother' ought to be construed in a reasonable sense, and, if the doctor is of the opinion, on reasonable grounds and with adequate knowledge, that the probable consequence of the continuance of the pregnancy will be to make the woman a physical or mental wreck, the doctor in such circumstances is operating for the purpose of preserving the life of the woman.

Parliament set the minimum age of marriage for a girl at 16, presumably on the view that it is very undesirable that a girl under the age of 16 should marry and have a child. The medical evidence given establishes that view. Apparently the pelvic bones are not set until a girl is 18, and it is an observation that appeals to one's common sense that it must be undesirable that a girl should go through the state of pregnancy, and, finally labour, when she is of tender years.

It is also necessary to consider the evidence about the effect of rape, especially on a child … It is only common sense that a girl who for 9 months has to carry in her body the reminder of the dreadful scene and then go through the pangs of childbirth must suffer great mental anguish. In view of the age of the girl and the fact that she had been raped with great violence, the operation ought to have been performed.

The doctor who has to decide the matter can only base his opinion on knowledge and experience, and, if he in good faith thinks that it is necessary for the purpose of preserving the life of the girl, then not only is he entitled to perform the operation but it is also his duty to do so.

… human life is sacred, and the protection that the law gives to human life is extended to the unborn child in the womb. The unborn child in the womb must not be destroyed unless that destruction ..of that child is for the purpose of preserving the yet more precious life of the mother.

Killing an unborn child

Section 212 of the Uganda Penal Code Act[7]

Under Section 212, any person who, when a woman is about to deliver a child, prevents the child from being born alive, through any unlawful act or omission, is guilty of an offence and is liable to imprisonment for life.

The purpose of Section 212

Section 212 covers a child who is capable of being born alive – about to be delivered.

The Section is intended to fill the gap between abortion – which deals with a foetus that could not survive outside the mother's body – and homicide. It provides for the conviction of a person who destroys a child in the process of birth, in circumstances where it could not be proved that the child had completely proceeded in a living state from its mother's body, so as to be in law, capable of being killed.[8] The offence under Section 212 requires the actual destruction of the child, whereas abortion is constituted by the act which attempts to procure a miscarriage.

When is a child capable of being born alive?

According to *Rance v Mid-Downs Health Authority* [1991] 1 All ER 801 and also *C v S* [1987] 1 All ER 1230 a child is capable of being born alive when it has reached such a stage of development in the womb that it is capable, if born then, of living and breathing through its lungs without any connection with its mother.

One can safely state that there is an obvious overlap between killing an unborn child and procuring a miscarriage.

---

1. Originally Section 206.
2. It is not uncommon for the prosecution to bring a charge of infanticide rather than murder whenever a woman kills her child who has not attained the age of 12 months. In such cases the prosecution does not adduce any evidence to support the defence and the defence usually does not find it in its favour to challenge the prosecution's case.
3. Collingwood J.J.R (1967) Criminal Law of East and Central Africa. London: Sweet and Maxwell. Lagos: African Universities Press.
4. Originally Section 136.
5. Originally Section 142.
6. Originally Section 143.
7. Originally Section 205.
8. Refer to section 190 which provides for when a child is deemed to be an object of homicide.

11
Involuntary manslaughter

'Generally, any unlawful homicide which is not classified as murder is manslaughter.' Card, Cross and Jones (1992:206). They continue:

> There are two generic types of manslaughter – voluntary and involuntary. A person is guilty of voluntary manslaughter where, although he has killed with malice aforethought, he has done so under circumstances which the law regards as mitigating the gravity of his offence.

Section 187 of the Uganda Penal Code Act

> 1. Any person who, by an unlawful act or omission, causes the death of another person is guilty of the felony termed manslaughter.
>
> 2. An unlawful omission is an omission amounting to culpable negligence to discharge a duty tending to the preservation of life or health, whether such omission is or is not accompanied by an intention to cause death or bodily harm.

All the homicides discussed so far deal with unlawful conduct accompanied with malice aforethought. Apart from murder and killings under Diminished Responsibility, all other homicides are legally regarded as manslaughter although they result from intentional killings. They are *voluntary* manslaughter since death is intended. Such are killings under provocation: killings in pursuance of suicide pacts as well infanticides. Although the killings are voluntary, they occur in circumstances which the law regards as mitigating the gravity of the crime. They are thus manslaughter and not murder.

Smith and Hogan (1992:365) refer to manslaughter cases not accompanied by malice aforethought as *involuntary manslaughter*. And Card, Cross and Jones (1992:206) define involuntary manslaughter as 'an unlawful killing where the accused has some blameworthy mental state less than an intention unlawfully to kill.'

The discussion which follows deals with the offence of manslaughter created under Section 187 of the Penal Code Act. Under section 187, death is caused by the accused, through an unlawful act or omission. The accused has some blameworthy mental state which is less than an intention to kill.

Causing death by unlawful act or omission (Section 187 (1))
Intention to cause grievous bodily harm
In the discussion of the concept of malice aforethought, it was revealed that where an accused's assault of the deceased was accompanied by an intention to cause grievous harm, rather than an intention to kill, but unfortunately death occurred, the offence is manslaughter and not murder. See *Bukenya v Uganda* and *Rujumba v Uganda* above.

Intoxication may negative presence of malice aforethought
Cases reveal that where evidence raises the probability that at the time of the killing, the accused was so intoxicated as not to be able to form the specific intent to kill, such

accused would be guilty of manslaughter only. See for example *Malungu s/o Kieti v R; Nyakite s/o Oyugi* above.

The use of excessive force

Cases discussed above have also revealed that where a person is entitled (by law) to use force, but uses more force than is necessary in the circumstances and thereby causes death, the courts will return a verdict of guilty of manslaughter. See for example cases discussed under what constitutes unlawful conduct such as: *Uganda v Abdu Muherwa; Marwa s/o Robi v R; Uganda v Bugga; Sharmpal Singh s/o Pritam Singh.*

Absence of common intention

Where in cases of mob justice, the prosecution proves that the different persons had a common intention to cause injury through beating but there is no proof that the parties had a common intention to kill through the beating, a verdict of manslaughter will be returned.

It is clear from case law that as long as there is doubt as to the existence of an intention to cause death, the doubt will be resolved in the accused's favour and she/he will be guilty of manslaughter and not murder. This is because malice aforethought is not presumed. It must be proved, and proved beyond reasonable doubt. Subsection (1) therefore covers cases where, although the conduct causing death was unlawful, the prosecution fails to prove beyond reasonable doubt that the *mens rea* which accompanied the conduct was intention to cause death, i.e. malice aforethought.

It can be concluded that the instances in which courts return verdicts of manslaughter greatly vary. In the case of *Andrews v Director of Public Prosecutions* [1937] 2 All ER 552 at 554, Lord Atkins expressed the uncertainty surrounding the offence of manslaughter:

> ... of all crimes, manslaughter appears to afford most difficulties of definition, for it concerns homicide in so many and so varying conditions.

Defining 'unlawful omission' (Section 187 (2))
What makes a negligent act culpable negligence?

In *Blyth v Birmingham Waterworks Co.* (1856) LR 11 Ex, it was stated that:

> Negligence is the omission to do something which a reasonable man, guided upon those considerations which ordinarily regulate the conduct of human affairs, would do, or doing something which a prudent and reasonable man would not do. (Per Alderson B at pg 784)

Lord Justice Bowen in *Thomas v Quartermane* (1887) 18 QBD at page 694 states:

> Negligence is simply neglect of some care which we are bound to exercise towards somebody.

In *Andrews v DPP* (1937) AC 576, The House of Lords said at page 47:

> The principle to be observed is that cases of manslaughter in driving motor cars are but instances of a general rule applicable to all charges of homicide. Simple lack of care such

as will constitute civil liability is not enough. For purposes of the criminal law, there are degrees of negligence, and a very high degree of negligence is required to be proved before the felony (manslaughter) is established. Probably of all epithets that can be applied 'reckless' most nearly covers the case. It is difficult to visualize a case of death caused by 'reckless' driving in the connotation of that term in ordinary speech which would not justify a conviction of manslaughter. But it is probably not all embracing for 'reckless' suggests an indifference to risk, whereas the accused may have appreciated the risk and intended to avoid it and yet shown such a high degree of negligence in the means adopted to avoid the risk as would justify a conviction.

In *R v Muinda* (1936-51) 6 U.L.R 163 it was held that a conviction of manslaughter ensues if the manner in which and the circumstances in which the accused drove the car would appear to the ordinary person to show that the accused when driving just before the accident, was callously indifferent to human life, then a conviction for manslaughter might ensue.

CASE: *Francis Ocoke v Uganda* (1992-3) HCB 43 (Supreme Court)
The appellant was convicted of murder under Section 183. He appealed against the conviction.The facts of the case were that the deceased was travelling on a tractor which was pulling a trailer. The deceased was sitting on the left side mudguard of the tractor. A lorry being driven by the appellant came at a terrific speed and knocked the trailer, thus disconnecting it from the tractor. The lorry then hit the right tyre of the tractor and the deceased was thrown down behind the tractor on its left side. The appellant stopped the lorry and reversed it between the tractor and the trailer and ran over the deceased, thus crushing him to death.

The appellant's defence was that the deceased was killed by accident. The trial judge rejected the defence and convicted the appellant of murder. He said:

It is well settled that in order to establish criminal liability based on negligence, the facts must be such that in the opinion of the court, the negligence of the accused went beyond a mere matter of compensation between subjects and showed such disregard for the life and safety of others as to amount to a crime against the state and conduct deserving punishment. See *R v Bateman* (1925) 19 Crim App Rep 8, *Andrews v DPP* (1937) A.C 576, (1938) 26 Crim App Rep 34. The degree of negligence must therefore be above that required to establish civil liability. It has been described variously as 'culpable', 'gross' or 'criminal'. The degree required to establish the offence of causing death by rash or negligent act is however lower than that required to establish manslaughter. See *James Phillip v R* (1952) 19 EACA 23.

In order to establish manslaughter, there must be a higher degree of negligence amounting to reckless disregard of human life. See *Andrews v DPP*; *R v Muinda* (1936-51) 6 U.L.R 163.

In the instant case the degree of negligence was so high as to establish an offence of manslaughter. The appellant's negligence consisted in overtaking at high speed, in hitting the trailer and the tractor and in reversing the lorry without taking due care to ensure that it was safe to do so and in the circumstances the appellant was guilty of manslaughter contrary to Section 182 of the Penal Code Act.

Result: Convicted of manslaughter.

12
Non-Fatal Assaults

Under Division IV (Offences Against the Person), the Penal Code creates different assaults and attaches different punishments depending on the nature or gravity of the harm suffered by the victim. In such offences against the person, the result of the injury is not death of a person. It is for this reason that I refer to them as non-fatal assaults.

It however needs to be noted that the different assaults are cognate and minor offences of murder and manslaughter. For example, a person may be accused of murder and the prosecution may be able to prove that the accused in fact assaulted the deceased and caused injuries on his/her body. But if they fail to prove beyond reasonable doubt, that the injuries caused by the accused were the cause of death, the accused would be guilty of assault occasioning actual bodily harm or grievous harm, but not murder.

In this respect the problem for the prosecution is to link the accused's actions directly with the death. See also examples under **Causation** (pp. 15-38).

CASE: In *Uganda v Mohammed Tembo & 2 Others* (1992-93) HCB 78, High Court. The accused were indicted for murder. It was alleged that they beat up the deceased and killed her. A post-mortem was not done so the size and nature of the wounds were not described. In murder cases, the cause of death must be established. Not all cut wounds lead to death. So although the accused were armed with lethal weapons, it was unsafe to conclude that the injuries sustained in the violence were the cause of her death and therefore conviction for murder or manslaughter could not be secured.

The accused were convicted of assault occasioning actual bodily harm.

In *Gichunge v R* [1972] E.A 546 it was held that unlawfully causing grievous harm is a complete minor offence in relation to murder. Although there was evidence to establish that the accused had assaulted the deceased, the prosecution did not link the resulting injuries to the death.

CASE: *Uganda v Kayingi Deograsiya & 4 Others* Criminal Session Case No. 60/ 1972 High Court.
The five accused were indicted for murder. Evidence clearly established that they had all taken part in unlawfully assaulting the deceased. Prosecution however failed to prove beyond reasonable doubt that the death of the deceased was a result of the assaults on him by the accused persons.

Held: The accused were guilty of the minor cognate offence of assault occasioning actual bodily harm.

Thus in a charge of murder where the prosecution proves that an accused caused bodily harm to the deceased but fail to prove beyond reasonable doubt that it was the injury caused by the accused that led to death, the accused can be convicted of grievous harm.

Common assault: Section 235 of the Uganda Penal Code[1]

Common assault occurs when a person (A) intentionally or recklessly causes another (V) to *apprehend* the application to his body of immediate and unlawful force or violence or discomfort. Apprehension – the expectation and fear of an assault - is an essential element of the crime. On the other hand, the victim need not in fact suffer the violence, for if he suffered violence, the conduct will be punished as another (more serious) form of assault.[2] Thus *Russell on Crime*, 12th ed., vol. 1 at p.652 said of assault:

> An assault, as distinct from battery, is a threat by one man to inflict unlawful force (whether light or heavy) upon another; it constitutes a crime at common law when the threatener, by some physical act, has intentionally caused the other to believe that such force is about to be inflicted upon him.

Under Section 235, what is being punished is the fact that (A) has created fear in (V), *not* that A has in fact injured (V).

Actus reus: The *actus reus* of common assault is: causing the victim to fear/apprehend the immediate application of force to his body.

Mens rea: The *mens rea* is the intention to cause in the victim apprehension of immediate unlawful violence, or recklessness as to whether such apprehension is caused. Negligence may amount to a tort but does not result into criminal liability.

Assault is also a tort and many principles appear to be equally applicable in both branches of the law.

Can words alone suffice to qualify as common assault?

Yes. For example, if the complainant is moving on the street and the accused moves towards him/her and says 'your bag or your life', even if the accused has not raised his hand in conduct which indicates that he is about to hit the complainant, the complainant may read a threat in the words and apprehend that the offender is implying that he is ready to use force to get the bag.

Another example of common assault through words can be if the complainant is walking down an alley and the accused goes behind the complainant and says 'Hit him boys'. Even if there are in fact no 'boys' to beat up the complainant, the complainant may imagine that some people are hiding within the immediate vicinity and that they are about to come out of their hiding place and beat him up.

If the law were different, it would 'deny the possibility of an assault in pitch darkness, when a gesture cannot be seen but menacing words can be heard.'

In *Wilson* [1955] 1 All ER 744, Lord Goddard said of the accused: 'He called out "Get out the knives" which in itself would be an assault, in addition to kicking the game keeper.'

Can threatening action without words be common assault?

One can commit common assault through a threatening action without any words and without contact. If the accused moved menacingly towards the complainant, with fists raised, such conduct may constitute common assault.

In *Stephen v Meyer* (1830) 4 C&P 349 it was held that a person may be guilty of an assault although he is prevented from touching the victim.

The complainant was a chairman at a meeting where he sat at the same table as the defendant but was separated from him by six or seven other people. The complainant ordered the defendant to leave the meeting on account of his disorderly behaviour, whereupon the defendant advanced towards the complainant with his fists clenched, saying that he would remove the complainant from the chair. Other people intervened before the defendant was near enough to the complainant to have hit him.

Chief Justice Tindall said:

> ... it is not every threat, where there is no actual personal violence, that constitutes an assault. There must be the means of carrying the threat into effect. In the instant case, although the defendant was not near enough to strike, he was advancing towards the complainant and if he had not been stopped, he would have hit the complainant. If he was so advancing, that, within a second or two ... he would have reached the victim, ... it is an assault in law.

Impossibility of carrying out a threat

If the circumstances are such that there cannot possibly be an immediate carrying out of the threat, then there is no assault. For example, if A is inside a fast moving train and when he sights V, who is standing at the side of the road, he menacingly shakes a fist as him. It is obvious that A cannot immediately hit V.

Intention to cause fear versus intention to hurt

For common assault to be proved, it is essential that fear was induced in the victim. If it is obvious that the threat cannot be carried out immediately, then that is not an assault. But what is important is the feelings of the victim, rather than whether the accused in actual fact intends to carry out the threat.

In *R v St George* (1840) 9 C & P 483 it was said that pointing an unloaded gun at another person amounts to common assault if the person at whom it is pointed does not know that it is unloaded.

Parke B said *inter alia*: if a person presents a pistol which has the appearance of being loaded, and puts the other party into fear and alarm, that is what it is the object of the law to prevent.

Thus where a person points an unloaded gun or a toy gun at another, and thereby induces fear in that other person, such conduct constitutes assault. As long as the victim is unaware of the harmlessness in the weapon, common assault has been committed.

See also *Kwaku Mensah v R* [1964] AC 83, PC.

Threat must be of immediate violence

It is clear that a threat to inflict harm at some time in the future cannot amount to an assault – an apprehension of immediate personal violence is essential.

In *Smith v Chief Superintendent, Woking Police Station.* (1983) 76 Crim App Rep 234, DC the Divisional Court took a generous view of what is 'immediate'. It held that where a woman was frightened by seeing the accused looking at her through the window of her bed-sitting room at 11 p.m., the accused was guilty of assault. The woman had apprehended the immediate application of force.

It is thus clear that common assault is an offence in which the *actus reus* is partly constituted by the effect the accused person's conduct has on the victim.

Unlawfulness is an ingredient in common assault

Section 227 provides that the assault must be unlawful before it constitutes an offence. If the word 'unlawfully' is not in the particulars of the offence, the charge becomes bad. The accused must be told that he assaulted the person named in the charge unlawfully.

In *Uganda v Abdu Bamuru* Crim Revision 330/1971 the accused was charged with assault c/s 227 P.C and the particulars alleged: 'On the 12th May 1971 ... Bamuru did assault Paulo'. The accused was convicted on his plea which was 'It is true that I assaulted the complainant.'

Because the actual word 'unlawfully' was not included, the case was dismissed.

Assault causing actual bodily harm: Section 236 Penal Code Act.[3]

Where a person intentionally or recklessly makes unlawful physical contact with the victim, such is assault occasioning actual bodily harm. The same offence is referred to as battery in English common law, an offence which constitutes the actual 'striking' of another person.

Section 236 deals with the actual infliction of unlawful personal violence by D upon P. There need be no apprehension of impending violence. What is important is that the offender succeeds in applying unlawful violence on another person.

Actus reus: The *actus reus* is the application of unlawful force and thereby causing harm to the body of another.

Mens rea: The element of *mens rea* is satisfied by proof that the accused either intentionally or recklessly applied unlawful force to the person of another. An intention to injure is not required. Bodily harm need not have been foreseen. Thus, the mens rea is merely that of an assault. Once the assault is proved, the only remaining question is one of occasion – was it the accused's assault that caused the harm?

No *mens rea* is required as to the injury. In *DPP v Parmenter* [1992] 1 AC 699 it was said that it is sufficient for the prosecution to show that the accused assaulted the victim and that as a matter of fact this caused actual bodily harm.

Defining harm

Under Section 2 of the Penal Code, harm is defined as 'any bodily hurt, disease or disorder whether permanent or temporary.' Section 236 covering actual bodily harm includes the smallest degree of personal contact, a mere touching without consent is technically an assault if it causes physical discomfort. There is, however, an implied consent to the degree of contact which is necessary or customary in everyday usage.

In *DPP v Smith* [1961] AC 290 the House of Lords said that actual bodily harm need not be really serious. The court distinguished bodily harm from grievous harm which was defined as 'really serious' harm.

In *Miller* [1954] 2 QB 282[4] Justice Lynskey said that 'actual bodily harm includes any hurt or injury calculated to interfere with the health or comfort of the victim. Such harm or injury need not be permanent, but must be more than transient or trifling'.

Actual bodily harm was defined in *R v Chan Fook* [1994] Crim LR as any injury which is more than trivial.Defi ni ng Harm
Under Section 2 of the Penal Code

CASE: *Roberts* (1971) 56 Crim App Rep 95... CA
The accused tried to remove the coat of a girl in a moving car, indicating that he meant to 'take liberties with her' against her will. The girl jumped out of the car and was injured. The accused appealed against conviction for assault occasioning actual bodily harm on the ground that the issue of whether the accused foresaw that the girl would jump and suffer injury, had not been considered.

The Court of Appeal rejected this, saying that the only issue was one of causation; the question was whether the victim's actions were the natural result of the accused's conduct, in the sense that they were something that could reasonably have been foreseen as the consequence of what the accused was saying or doing.

Actual bodily harm is a question of fact

Whether the complainant sustained actual bodily harm is a question of fact, to be determined by the court on the evidence available – High Court of Uganda in *Uganda v Mohammed Tembo & 2 Others* (1992-93) HCB 78.

Most assaults causing actual bodily harm are directly inflicted, e.g. A strikes P with his fist or with a weapon. But it is not necessary that the violence is directly inflicted. Therefore, if A sets a dog on P, A will still be guilty of the resulting injury even if he did not directly touch the victim.

Cases and rulings on actual bodily harm

Uganda v Mohammed Tembo and Others 1992-1993 HCB 78
Held *inter alia* that:

> Whether the complainant in a case sustained actual bodily harm is a question of fact to be decided by the court on the evidence available. In the instant case the deceased sustained a cut wound on the head and her body was covered with blood. The accused persons were therefore guilty of assault occasioning actual bodily harm.

R v Msungwe [1968] EA203
The accused first assaulted the complainant and then chased him with a knife. Whilst running away from the accused the complainant tried to jump over a furrow but fell and broke his leg. The accused left him lying semi-conscious. Eventually the complainant was taken to hospital and had his leg amputated. The accused was convicted of doing grievous harm.

On revision a question was raised: Whether the conviction could be supported when the injury to the complainant was not caused directly by the accused.

Held: The conviction was proper (*R v Halliday* applied). Justice Biron said:

> ... the injury was caused by the complainant's attempting to jump over the furrow in fleeing from the accused. Even in the absence of any authority I would agree with the learned trial magistrate who said 'Although the accused did not hit in order to break the leg of the complainant, he technically did so by setting the motion of the whole system which resulted into a grave injury on the complainant's leg. The complainant was at a big dilemma. If he stood within the reach of the accused he would no doubt have been knifed. He decided to run in escape, which is a natural thing, he fell into the ditch thereby losing his leg.

Republic v Cheya & Another [1973] EA 500: Assault occasioning actual bodily harm is a cognate minor offence to murder.

Defences to assault occasioning actual bodily harm

1. Consent
2. Lawful correction

Consent

Consent negates the crime and the onus of proving the absence of consent is on the prosecution. Consent to harm is allowed by the law if the intended harm serves some public interest or good. Examples are:

1. Surgical operations necessarily involve harm but the harm is done for a valuable purpose.
2. In properly conducted games or sports, such as boxing, wrestling, etc. there is some minimum level of accepted violence. However, although a person who participates in a properly conducted game consents to the risk of actual bodily harm, he/she only consents to such harm as may be incidental to the game in question, and not to any other type of harm. (*Donovan* [1934] 2 KB 498)

Cases and rulings on consent

Christopherson v Barke (1848) 11 QB 473: It is of the essence of a conviction that the act resulting in the harm was done against the will of the victim.

R v Venna 1976 1 QB 421: It will be a defence to a charge of causing actual bodily harm that the accused had the victim's express or implied consent.

R v Donovan [1934] 2 KB 489: The use of force by one person against another is only criminal if done without the consent of such other person. The onus of proving its absence rests upon the prosecution.

Limitations on consent

There are limits to the right of any person to consent to the infliction of physical harm on him/herself. Under Section 226 of the Penal Code it is provided that consent by a person to the causing of his or her own death or his or her own maim does not affect the criminal responsibility of any person by whom such death or maim is caused.[5]

In *R v Donovan* [1934] 2 KB 489 it was ruled that:

Consent is no defence to a charge of doing an act which is likely, or intended to do serious bodily harm..

It is no defence to a charge of murder for the accused to say that P asked to be killed. On the other hand, P's consent to D's taking a high degree of risk of killing him/her is effective where it is justified by the purpose of the act, e.g in the case of a surgical operation. Where the act has some social purpose recognised by the law as valid, it is a question of balancing the degree of harm which will or may be caused against the value of that purpose. But consent is only operative if it is for a purpose recognised as valid by the law e.g surgical operations but not abortion.[6]

Lawful corrections

Under English common law, parents and other persons in *loco parentis* are entitled to inflict moderate and reasonable physical chastisement on their children. According to *Cleary v Booth* [1893] 1 QB 465, such persons are entitled, as a disciplinary measure, to apply a reasonable degree of force to their children, old enough to understand its purpose. See also *Donovan* [1934] 2 KB 498

But 'if it be administered for the gratification of passion or rage or if it be immoderate or excessive in its nature or degree,[7] or if it be protracted beyond the child's powers of endurance or with an instrument unfitted for the purpose and calculated to produce danger to life and limb, then it is unlawful.' *Hopley* (1860) 2 F&F 202.

Smith and Hogan (1992:411) have also stated that the position at common law was that:

If the chastisement is moderate, it would be impracticable for the courts to inquire very closely into the validity of the parent's motives. Where the force is immoderate, his motives are irrelevant.

Card, Cross and Jones (1992:180) reported that under common law:

Parents and other persons in *loco parentis* are entitled as a disciplinary measure to apply a reasonable degree of force to their children or charges old enough to understand its purpose. However, if the corporal punishment is given out of spite or anger, or for some other non-disciplinary reason, or if the degree of force is unreasonable, it is unlawful.

Thus, beyond that which is 'reasonable' a parent would be prosecuted under criminal law and punished according to the nature of the injury inflicted on the child.

Under English common law, school teachers are in the same position as parents with regard to the conduct of the child at, or on its way to or from school.[8]

Under common law, it is not for the parent to prove that the force used was lawful. It is for the prosecution to prove beyond reasonable doubt that the force was *not* lawful. Thus if a parent is prosecuted for having applied physical force on his/her child, and he/she claims that the force was used for correction, he/she must be acquitted unless the prosecution proves that the force used was unreasonable, or disproves some other element relevant to the claim.

Corporal punishment and children's human rights

Is the use of corporal punishment by parents and those in the position of parents still legal within the discourse of children's rights? What rights do the use of corporal punishment violate?

The issue has been succinctly put by the Global Initiative to end all Corporal Punishment of Children, (2002:1)[9] thus:

> Corporal punishment of children breaches their fundamental human rights to respect for human dignity and physical integrity. Its legality in almost every state world wide – in contrast to other forms of interpersonal violence – challenges the universal right to equal protection under the law.

And in the words of John Hunt (2002:1),[10] the most important reason for banning the physical punishment of children is that:

> … all people have the right to protection of their physical integrity, and children are people too.

A discussion of corporal punishment of children within a human rights discourse calls for analysis of Articles 19(1); 28(2) and 37(a) of the United Nations Convention on the Rights of the Child (CRC). Similar provisions are found in Articles 11(5), 16(1) of the African Charter on the Rights and Welfare of the Child (the African Child Charter). Under Article 19(1) of the CRC, it is provided that:

> States Parties shall take all appropriate legislative, administrative, social and educational measures to protect the child from all forms of physical or mental violence, injury or abuse … while in the care of parents, legal guardian(s) or any other person who has the care of the child.

A similar provision is found under Article 16(1) of the African Child Charter:

> States Parties to the present Charter shall take specific legislative, administrative, social and educational measures to protect the child from all forms of torture, inhuman or degrading treatment and especially physical or mental injury or abuse …

Article 28(2) CRC states that:

> States Parties shall take all appropriate measures to ensure that school discipline is administered in a manner consistent with the child's human dignity and in conformity with the present Convention.

In a similar vein, Article 11(5) of the African Child Charter provides that:

> States Parties to the present Charter shall take all appropriate measures to ensure that a child who is subjected to school or parental discipline shall be treated with humanity and with respect for the inherent dignity of the child and in conformity with the present Charter.

Similarly, Article 20(1) (c) of the African Child Charter states that:

> Parents or other persons responsible for the child shall have the primary responsibility of the upbringing and development of the child and shall have the duty to ensure that domestic discipline is administered with humanity and in a manner consistent with the inherent dignity of the child.

And under Article 37(a) of the CRC, it is provided that:

> States Parties shall ensure that no child shall be subjected to torture or other cruel, inhuman or degrading treatment or punishment.

In summary, the relevant provisions enjoin states to ensure that children are protected from practices which expose them to abuse and violence which could lead to physical and mental injury. The articles also protect children from treatment which ignores the fact that children, by virtue of being human beings, are entitled to be treated with dignity and respect. Although the provisions acknowledge the need to discipline children, the articles make it clear that even when parents or school authorities administer disciplinary measures against children, they are bound by the need to ensure a child's personal integrity.

Is corporal punishment a form of abuse, is it a form of violence?

Physical abuse occurs when a person deliberately inflicts physical harm on the body of another. Physical abuse of children refers to non-accidental physical injury of a child by a parent or any other caretaker. In the context of corporal punishment, the parent's primary intention is not to hurt the child for its own sake, but to correct or discipline the child through pain. What makes corporal punishment abusive is not the intention of the parent but rather the consequent negative impact of its application, which is often not limited to physical pain but extends to mental/psychological injury – humiliation, degradation, etc.

A lot of literature on corporal punishment asserts that it is a form of abuse, that it is violence against children and that it is inhuman and degrading treatment or punishment. The Committee on the Rights of the Child, which is responsible for making authoritative interpretations of the rights contained in the CRC, and for reviewing the compliance of states parties, has stated categorically that all forms of corporal punishment are incompatible with the protections given to children under the convention. The committee has criticised governments for permitting corporal punishment in schools and has stated repeatedly that corporal punishment violates the fundamental principles of the CRC. The committee has understood Articles 19 and 28 as imposing a requirement on states to prohibit corporal punishment in schools. In its official report of its seventh session in November 1994, the committee stated that:

> In the framework of its mandate, the Committee has paid particular attention to the child's right to physical integrity. In the same spirit it has stressed that corporal punishment of children is incompatible with the Convention and has often proposed the revision of existing legislation, as well as the development of awareness and education campaigns, to prevent ... the physical punishment of children.

The committee members, and indeed many scholars and child rights activists have argued that the difficulties in drawing sharp lines between acceptable and unacceptable forms of corporal punishment require a total ban on the practice, since even ostensibly mild forms of corporal punishment in practice often become severely abusive.

In a concluding statement to the general discussion on 'Children's Rights in the Family' in October 1994, committee member Thomas Hammarberg of Sweden noted that:

Certain states have tried to distinguish between the correction of children and excessive violence. In reality the dividing line between the two is artificial. It is very easy to pass from one stage to another.

Does corporal punishment humiliate or degrade a person?
Article 24 of Uganda's Constitution provides that:

> No person shall be subjected to any form of torture, cruel, inhuman or degrading treatment or punishment.

In my view, degradation refers to a lowering of somebody's standing. This can be in terms of how others regard that person, and/or how one regards oneself.

Uganda's Constitutional Court has declared the use of corporal punishment on anybody convicted on an offence, unconstitutional for violating a person's right to protection from cruel, inhuman and degrading treatment.[11] In 1995, the Ministry of Education issued a ban against corporal punishment in schools. It is, however, known that the use of the cane is still prevalent in many schools. The Uganda Human Rights Commission also considers corporal punishment at school as inhuman, degrading treatment. The Commission has however shied away from making a similar rule in relation to corporal punishment by parents.

The way forward
The concept of public interest litigation has taken firm root and is now accepted by the Uganda judiciary. Perhaps it is high time child rights activists brought the issue to court for declaration. World over, there have been various landmark judgements, quoting human rights principles and condemning corporal punishment of children, both in schools and within the family. Hopefully, our court will be guided by the High Court of Delhi, which, like the Uganda court, was faced by the English common law rule expounded in *R v Hopley* (1860). A petition was brought by the *Parents' Forum For Meaningful Education* and its President, Kusum Jain. The petition challenged the legality of corporal punishment in schools. The petition succeeded and the High Court of Delhi, in a judgement delivered on December 1, 2000 directed the state to ensure 'that children are not subjected to corporal punishment in schools and they receive education in an environment of freedom and dignity, free from fear'.

The Government, defending the use of corporal punishment, quoted English common law and referred to the leading case of *R v Hopley* which held that a parent or schoolteacher had a right to use 'reasonable and moderate' corporal punishment. Referring to *Hopley*, the judge said:

> It may be noted that this decision was rendered about one and a half centuries back. Since then thinking has undergone a sea of .change. The United Nations Convention ... is a testimony of that change and the importance which is being attached to the child. Law cannot be static. It must move with the time.

It is also noted that the Committee on the Rights of the Child has condemned legal concepts, which attempt to define 'acceptable' violence towards children, 'reasonable chastisement', etc.

As long as we agree that the use of corporal punishment has human rights implications, declaring as void laws that give it validity will be an automatic conclusion. Thus in 1996, the Supreme Court of Italy declared corporal punishment for educational purposes unlawful and said:

> ... There are two reasons for this: the first is the overriding importance, which the [Italian] legal system attributes to protecting the dignity of the individual. This includes 'minors' who now hold rights and are no longer simply objects to be protected by their parents or, worse still, objects at the disposal of their parents.

In the year 2000, the Supreme Court of Israel declared all corporal punishment, however light, unlawful. After quoting Article 19 CRC, the leading judge noted inter alia that:

> It may be argued that this ruling is one that the community will be unable to bear, for many parents make use of force that is not disproportionate in nature against their children.

Nevertheless, the judge concluded:

> ...Corporal punishment of children, or humiliation and derogation from their dignity as a method of education by their parents, is entirely impermissible, and is a remnant of a societal-educational outlook that has lost its validity. The child is not the parent's property and cannot be used as a punching bag the parents can beat at their leisure, even when the parents honestly believe that they are fulfilling their duty and right to educate their child. The child depends upon the parents, is entitled to parental love, protection and the parents' gentle touch. The use of punishment, which causes hurt and humiliation, does not contribute to the child's personality or education, but instead damages his or her human rights. Such punishment injures his or her body, feelings, dignity and proper development ... parents are now forbidden to make use of corporal punishment or methods that demean and humiliate the child.[12]

There is a need to be reminded that the right to protection from degrading treatment or punishment is unqualified. According to Article 44 of Uganda's Constitution:

> Notwithstanding anything in this constitution, there shall be no derogation from the enjoyment of the following rights and freedoms: a) freedom from torture, cruel, inhuman or degrading treatment or punishment.

If a person who has infringed the provisions of criminal law is protected from degrading punishment, there is no justification for allowing a child who has infringed social rules to suffer degradation.

Many pro-corporal punishment groups will put forward the *positive* side of the practice. But the need to emphasise the human rights paradigm of corporal punishment on children clearly comes out in the position paper on corporal punishment by the Global Initiative to End All Corporal Punishment of Children (2002:3):

> ... People forget the human rights imperative for action now: we do not look into the effects of physical discipline on women, or on animals. It is enough that it breaches fundamental rights. Finding some positive short or long-term effects of corporal punishment would not reduce the human rights imperative for banning it.

According to Article 44 of the Constitution, the right to be protected from degrading and inhuman treatment is absolute.

Doing Grievous Harm: Section 219 of the Uganda Penal Code Act.[13]

> Any person who unlawfully does grievous harm to another is guilty of a felony and is liable to imprisonment for 7 years.

What constitutes grievous harm?

According to Section 2: 'grievous harm' means any harm which amounts to a maim or dangerous harm, or seriously or permanently injures health or which is likely so to injure health, or which extends to permanent disfigurement, or to any permanent or serious injury to any external or internal organ, membrane or sense.[14]

Must the victim be wounded?

Grievous bodily harm may cover cases where there is no wounding, e.g a broken bone. Conversely, there might be a technical 'wounding' which could not be said to amount to grievous bodily harm.

In *DPP v Smith* [1961] AC 290 the House of Lords defined grievous harm as 'really serious' harm.

> A person charged with causing grievous harm can be convicted of assault occasioning actual bodily harm since actual bodily harm is a cognate but lesser offence of grievous harm. The only difference between the two offences is the nature of injury suffered by the victim.

Whatever the nature of assault, an assault will be unlawful if it is carried out without consent and without lawful excuse

Note: Whether a resulting injury constitutes grievous harm or just harm is a question of fact. What is important is that the trial court gives serious thought to the nature of injury as presented by the available evidence. The best evidence for guidance is medical evidence. If the medical officer's report gives details such as the depth of the wound, etc., such detail would guide the court in determining whether to convict under Section 228 or under Section 212. Where there is doubt as to whether the nature of injury falls under Section 212 or 228, the benefit of doubt works in the accused's favour and the conviction would have to be under the lesser offence: actual bodily harm.

CASE: *Uganda v Charles Akaku* (1992-93) HCB 49 (High Court)
The accused was charged and convicted of causing grievous bodily harm contrary to Section 212.

Held: Losing a tooth is not grievous harm within the meaning of Section 4 and therefore the accused should not have been convicted of causing grievous bodily harm.

CASE: *Uganda v Monoko & 2 Others* [1985] HCB 16 (High Court)
The accused assaulted the complainant and as a result of the assault, 8 of the complainant's teeth had to be removed. The trial magistrate following *Uganda v Egoru* 1976 HCB 187 convicted the accused of assault occasioning actual bodily harm and observed: 'To me this seems an unfortunate decision but I am bound by it.'

Held on revision:

1. The medical assistant/dental assistant was competent to classify the injury as grievous harm as he was specifically trained in dental care. He was therefore able to assess the gravity of the injury sustained by the victim. The accused should therefore have been convicted for grievous harm.
2. The assault inflicted on the victim was grievous harm within the meaning of section 4 of the Penal Code as removal of 8 teeth extends to permanent disfigurement of the victim. Whereas some people in some areas of Uganda may voluntarily remove their teeth as a sign of beauty, some other people in Uganda regard their teeth as very precious and so loss of their teeth is a deformity which has undesirable permanent ugly features on the victim which brings the injury within the meaning of Section 4 of the Penal Code. Each case should be decided on its own facts, taking into account all the surrounding circumstances of the case including the value and importance which a given people may attach to its teeth.

CASE: *Uganda v Pampara* [1991] HCB 16 (High Court)

The appellant, a teacher, subjected the complainant, a pupil in his school, to corporal punishment. A medical doctor who examined the complainant classified the injuries inflicted on the body as harm and the injury to the eye, that is conjunctivitis and cornea, as grievous harm.

Issue: Whether the offence of grievous harm had been proved.

Held *inter alia*:
1. Section 4 of the Penal Code defines 'grievous harm' as meaning any harm which amounts to a maim or dangerous harm, or seriously or permanently injures health or which is likely so to injure health, or which extends to permanent disfigurement, or to any permanent or serious injury to any external or internal organ, membrane or sense.
2. The medical doctor who testified rightly classified the injuries on the cornea and conjunctivitis as grievous harm because they were injuries to the external organ responsible for sight. The trial magistrate accepted the doctor's expert opinion and rightly found that the injuries constituted grievous harm as defined under section 4 of the penal Code Act.

CASE: *Uganda v George Ogwang* Criminal Revision No. 43 of 1978 (High Court)

The accused struck the complainant with a handle of a hoe on her right hand and she sustained a fracture of her little finger. She was examined by a Senior Medical Assistant who gave evidence that the injury was consistent with a blow by a blunt object and he classified the injury as grievous harm. The trial magistrate convicted the accused of doing grievous harm under Section 212 of the Penal Code.

Held: On revision, it was held *inter alia* that:
1. The learned trial magistrate should have given the matter more serious attention in order to determine whether the injury inflicted amounted to grievous harm as defined in Section 4 of the Penal Code.

3. A mere fracture of a little finger does not amount to grievous harm, it amounts to harm only.

Conclusion: A court should give serious thought to the nature of injury suffered by a victim of an assault before determining whether the harm falls under Sections 236 or 219 Penal Code.

CASE: *Bukenya v Uganda* 1967 EA 341 (High Court)
The appellant was charged with assault causing grievous bodily harm under Section 212 of the Penal Code. A medical report on the complainant was submitted but the magistrate made no comment on the report, did not admit it as an exhibit and convicted the appellant on his own plea which was 'I did give her injuries on her body.'

Held:
1. The statement 'I did give her injuries on her body' did not amount to an unequivocal plea of guilty to the charge having regard to the ingredients necessary to constitute the offence.
2. The magistrate erred in not admitting the medical report as an exhibit, as the medical evidence was indispensable for the purpose of establishing whether the injury was grievous harm or just ordinary hurt or no harm at all.

Result: Appeal allowed.

Intention to harm
Mens rea: Section 219 does not directly refer to the accused's state of mind; it is not specifically mentioned that the accused must maliciously or intentionally cause the harm, it only refers to unlawfully causing the harm.

CASE: *Gitau v R* [1961] EA 449
The appellants were convicted of unlawfully doing grievous harm. One of the grounds for appeal was that there was no intent to cause grievous harm

Held:
The word 'unlawfully' covers reckless and grossly negligent acts. An intention to cause harm is unnecessary. There is no need for the prosecution to prove that the accused intended to cause grievous harm.

A man must be taken to have intended the consequences of his acts
CASE: *Martin* (1881) 8 QBD 54
Shortly before the end of a performance in a theatre, Martin put out the lights and placed an iron bar across the doorway. In the ensuing panic to get out of the building, several people were injured. There was no evidence that Martin was motivated by ill will towards anyone. Martin was convicted of inflicting grievous bodily harm.

Held *inter alia* that: The harm was as truly inflicted by Martin as if he had hurled a stone at the victim. A man must be taken to have intended the natural consequences of that which he did. Thus a man can be convicted under the section even where he was merely acting mischievously.

Self-defence in non-fatal assaults

Self-defence may afford a defence not only to murder, as discussed earlier, but also to lesser offences such as assault occasioning actual bodily harm (and grievous bodily harm)[15]. It is subject to similar conditions. An attack which would not justify a killing in self-defence might justify the use of lesser degree of force and so afford a defence to a charge of actual bodily harm. But just as in homicide, if the person uses greater force than is reasonable to repel the attack, he or she may be guilty of assault causing actual or grievous bodily harm. Reasonable force may be used in defence of property, as well as in the arrest of an offender.

CASE: *James Owino v Uganda* [1977] 54

The appellant was charged with and convicted of assault occasioning actual bodily harm. He appealed to the High Court against conviction and sentence.

The prosecution alleged that the complainant went to a house of one Omondi to collect his property and there he found the appellant who cut him with a panga. The appellant admitted having cut the complainant but said that he did so because the complainant wanted to kill him. The trial magistrate disbelieved the appellant.

Held: High Court held that:

1. A defence of self-defence in an assault charge is recognised by law and an attack upon a person may be repelled by use of reasonable force. But the use of greater force than is reasonable to repel the attack will result in liability to conviction for common assault or whatever offence the degree of harm caused and intended warrants. *Morse* (1910) 4 Crim App Rep 50
2. If a threat of an assault is held out, there must in all cases be the means of carrying out the threat into effect.
3. In the instant case there was no evidence to show that the complainant was armed with any weapon with which he was alleged to have threatened to kill the appellant and therefore the defence of self-defence could not be raised.

Reasonable force may be used in arresting an offender

Section 24: The person arrested shall not be subjected to more restraint than is necessary to prevent his escape.

CASE: In *Beard v Republic* [1970] EA 448 the court referred to the law governing the rights of a member of the public to affect an arrest and the duties attached to the exercise of that power. Court cited Sections 21 and 24 of the Kenya Criminal Procedure Code which provide that:

1. In making an arrest the police officer or other person making the same shall actually touch or confine the body of the person to be arrested, unless there be a submission to the custody by word or action.
2. If such person forcibly resists the endeavour to arrest him, or attempts to evade the arrest, such police officer or other person may use all means necessary to effect the arrest.
3. Nothing in this section shall be deemed to justify the use of greater force than was reasonable in the particular circumstances in which it was employed or was necessary for the apprehension of the offender.

Held *inter alia*:

1. Where a suspect submits to custody, there is no justification to touch him and/ or use any force towards him.
2. Where force is used against a person who has submitted to custody, the force used constitutes an unlawful assault (and the person effecting the arrest would be guilty of either causing actual bodily harm or grievous harm depending on the nature of injuries visited on the body of the person arrested).

The above refers to cases of lawful arrest. However, if a person is *unlawfully* detained, he or she is entitled to resist the detention even with violence and would not be guilty of assault.

CASE: *Nzige Juma v R* [1964] EA
The appellant was convicted of assaulting a police officer in due execution of his duty. The evidence was that a police sergeant suspected the appellant of having in his possession drugs stolen or unlawfully obtained. When the policeman tried to detain and search the appellant, the appellant assaulted him. The appellant was not given any reason for his detention and search but evidence showed that he knew the reason.

On appeal one of the questions was: Whether the detention and intended search were lawful?

Held *inter alia*: The omission or failure of the police officer to inform the appellant why he was being detained and searched did not render his conduct unlawful as the appellant knew the reasons for the search and the police officer was not given any opportunity to explain to the appellant his reason for the search.
As the police officer's conduct was lawful, the appellant was properly convicted.
He could not plead self-defence. Justice Biron said:

> Unless the police officer's conduct was lawful, detention of the accused and search would constitute wrongful imprisonment and an assault, which the appellant would be entitled to resist even to the extent of using violence.

As noted by the High Court in *Uganda v Ello* 1977 HCB 232, assault occasioning actual bodily harm is a cognate but lesser offence of grievous harm. Thus where it is proved that an accused assaulted and injured the complainant, but the injuries are not classified, and the court is not certain whether the injuries were grievous or dangerous, the court will return a verdict of occasioning actual bodily harm. See *Francis Sebanenya, Petero Kabafumu* v *Uganda* Criminal Appeal No.17/1989 (Supreme Court).

Assault occasioning actual bodily harm is a cognate minor offence to murder. See *Republic v Cheya & Another* [1973] EA500

Criminal Law and HIV/AIDS

World over there is widespread debate on the appropriateness of using criminal sanctions to prosecute people who engage in activities that risk transmitting HIV. Reports of incidences (however rare they may be) of deliberate transmission of HIV/AIDS lead to public calls for the use of criminal law. Two major issues arise:

1. Criminalisation of deliberate or negligent harmful behaviour by persons with HIV/AIDS
2. The question of compulsory HIV testing of sexual offenders and the effect of an offender's HIV status in arriving at the sentence.

This section deals with the first issue and its relevance to homicides and non-fatal assaults.

Proponents of criminalisation argue that HIV-positive people who place others at risk of infection should be criminally prosecuted, because it is necessary to punish and deter such conduct. Such people must be held accountable for their irresponsible behaviour.

On the other hand, other groups argue that the use of criminal law is unlikely to be effective. Where behaviour is spontaneous and driven by human passion, as is sexual behaviour,[16] it is unlikely that the possibility of punishment will have a meaningful effect on people's behaviour. History indicates that punitive policies are counterproductive in the promotion of public health issues. Criminal prosecutions are not only unlikely to deter risky sex but will instead deter those most at risk from getting tested. The anti-criminalisation lobby also bases its stand on the human rights implications of the suggested criminalisation for people infected with HIV/AIDS.

A discussion on the role of criminal law in the management of the AIDS pandemic, especially from a human rights perspective, is too wide a topic to exhaustively handle in this book. Here, however, we raise some questions which will enable the student of criminal law to give thought to issues that continuously engages criminal lawyers:

1. Is it possible to punish individuals who, knowing that they are HIV-positive, engage in behaviours that can transmit HIV without using precautions and without informing their partners about their HIV status?
2. Is it possible to use existing provisions of the Uganda Penal Code to punish 'offenders' e.g. causing grievous harm, attempted murder, murder and manslaughter already discussed above? What about Section 227?[17] Or would there be a need to create a specific provision criminalising the relevant conduct?

The United Nations HIV/AIDS and Human Rights International Guidelines identify four different elements that need to be established clearly to justify criminal sanctions: *foreseeability, intent, causality, and consent.*

1. *Foreseeability:* To establish the criminal transmission of HIV the prosecution must prove that at the time of sexual intercourse, the accused knew or had reason to believe that he/she was HIV positive. The accused must also be aware that the virus is harmful and that it is capable of being transmitted to another through sexual intercourse.
2. *Intent:* what kind of *mens rea* will be adequate, must it be intention, recklessness or even negligence? It is imperative that laws relating to criminal transmission are used judiciously. They should criminalise the *wilful* transmission of HIV and not the HIV positive status of a person. The relevant *mens rea* must be clearly established so as not to punish the accused simply because of the act of transmission.
3. *Causality:* If the law is to punish only instances in which transmission *in fact* occurs then for the offence of criminal transmission the prosecution must

establish that the victim/complainant was infected by the accused. The prosecution must prove that the complainant was HIV negative at the time she/he engaged in sexual activity with the accused. It must be proved that the complainant was infected by the accused and not by anybody else. Securing a conviction may prove difficult, mainly due to the specific characteristics of the disease, i.e. its long incubation period and its invisibility. This makes establishing a causal link between an incident of transmission to one particular accused difficult. Although it is now possible through use of properly equipped and staffed DNA analysis to tell with some certainty whether the victim's HIV came from a particular source, the process is too expensive for Uganda. However the law may punish a person who wilfully engages in conduct which exposes another to the risk of infection even where the complainant escapes infection. This can be a specific offence or such behaviour can be punished according to the principles of attempts to commit a crime. The law would thus focus on criminal offences that prohibit behaviour which either results in transmission of disease or puts people at risk of contracting disease.

4. *Consent:* Would informed consent be a defence to a criminal charge? If A reveals his/her HIV status to B and B nevertheless consents to unprotected sexual activity with A this would perhaps offer a defence to A in the event of B being infected by A. So what constitutes informed consent is not that B willingly had sex with A but that B knew that A was HIV positive and willingly agreed to have unprotected sex with him/her. In the case of *R v Cuerrier*[18] Cuerrier had unprotected sex with women without disclosing what he knew to be his HIV infection. The Supreme Court of Canada unanimously held: Without disclosure of HIV status there cannot be true consent. The consent cannot simply be to have sexual intercourse. Rather it must be consent to have it with a partner who is HIV positive.

A further issue also needs to be considered: If an accused does not reveal his/her HIV status but takes precautions such as the use of a condom to protect his/her partner, but nevertheless transmission occurs what would his/her criminal responsibility be?

---

1. Originally Section 227.
2. It is the nature or gravity of injury that will determine the specific nature of asault that an offender will b epunished for, once the victim suffers violence or injury.
3. Originally Section 228 and phrased as "assault occasioning actual bodily harm"
4. [1954] 2 All ER 529
5. See discussion on Aiding suicide (Section 202) and Suicide Pacts (Section 188B) of the Penal Code Act.
6. Re-visit discussion on procuring miscarriage.
7. Thus if it results into grievous bodily harm rather than mere actual bodily harm, it becomes criminal.
8. Cleary v Booth [1893] 465; Newport (Salop)jj [1929] 2 KB 416; Mansell v Griffin [1908] 1 KB 160
9. http://endcorporalpunishment.org/pages/intro/intro.html. Accessed on 2/14/02

10. 'Ten Reasons Not to Hit Your Kids.' http://www.naturalchild.com/jan – hunt/ tenreasons.html. Accessed on 26/01/02.

11. *Kyamanywa Simon versus Uganda*, Constitutional Reference No. 10 of 2000.

12. unofficial translation: Israel Supreme Court, Criminal Appeal 4596/98 Plonit v A.G 54(1)P.D.P. 145.

13. Originally Section 212.

14. Originally Section 4.

15. The offence of grievous bodily harm is to be discussed later.

16. In Uganda HIV/AIDS is predominantly spread through heterosexual penetrative sex and for this reason my brief discussion on the topic will not make any references to the sharing of needles by "drug users".

17. Any person who by any rash or negligent act, not amounting to manslaughter, causes the death of another person is liable to imprisonment …

18(1998) 162 DLR (4th) 513

Bibliography

Alford M.: Euthanasia. http://www.jmu.edu/evision/archive/volume2/essays/alford.html. Accessed 30.9.2003.

Card, Cross and Jones (1992): *Criminal Law* (12th ed). London, Dublin, Edinburgh. Butterworths.

Collingwood (1967): *Criminal Law of EastAfrica and Central Africa.* London, Sweet and Maxwell; Lagos, African Universities Press.

Criminal Law Lecture Notes 1998/1999: *Homicide: An overview.* http://privatewww.essex.ac.uk~joash/homicide.htm. Accessed on 28/10/02

Criminal Procedure Code Act, Chapter 121 Laws of Uganda. Revised Edition 2000.

Curzon, L.B. (1997): *Criminal Law,* 8th ed, Pitman.

'Global Initiative to end all Corporal Punishment of Children' (2002): http://endcorporalpunishment.org/pages/inro.html. Accessed on 14/2/02.

Kirby, Michael (2000): *Through the World's Eye.* Law, Ethics and Public Affairs series.

Makubuya, Apollo (2000): 'The Constitutionality of the Death Penalty in Uganda: a critical Inquiry'. *East African Journal of Peace and Human Rights.* Vol.6, nr 2, pp.222-225.

Morris and Read (1966): Customary Law under Colonial Rule, London, Stevens and Sons.

Perkins and Boyce: Criminal Law (3rd edition), Foundation Press.

Pretty v The United Kingdom: http://www.echr.coe.int.

Smith and Hogan (1992): *Criminal Law* (7th ed), London, Dublin, Edinburgh, Butterworths.

'Ten Reasons not to hit your Kids': http://www/nauralchild.com/jan-hunt/tenreasons.html. Accessed on 26/1/02.

The Constitution of the Republic of Uganda (Revised Edition 2000): Chapter 1: 'Laws of Uganda'.

The Convention against Torture and Other Cruel, Inhuman or Degrading Treatment or Punishment. Unga Resolution 39/46, December 10, 1984.

The European Convention on Human Rights.

The International Covenant on Civil and Political Rights (ICCPR), 1966.

The Penal Code Act (Revised Editiion 2000): Chapter 120, 'Laws of Uganda'.

The Second Optional Protocol to the ICCPR (1998).

The Trial on Indictments Decree: Chapter122 Laws of Uganda (revised edition 2000).

The Witchcraft Act: Chapter 123, Laws of Uganda (Revised Edition 2000).

Tumwine-Mukubwa (2000): 'The Promotion and Protection of Human Rights in East Africa', *East African Journal of Peace and Human Rights,*

Glossary of Legal Terms

Actus reus: Guilty act. The *actus reus* is the act which, in combination with a certain menal state, constitutes a crime.

Corpus delecti: Body of the crime. Used to describe physical evidence of the corpse of a murder victim.

De minimus: The law does not care about very small matters.

In loco parentis: In the role of parents.

In rerum natura: In the nature of things.

Mens rea: The mental element of a crime.

Novus actus interveniens: A new intervening act.

Pari materia: Of the same matter, on the same subject.

Per curium: By the court. Defines a decision of an appeals court as a whole, in which no judge is identified as the specific author.

Per se: By itself, inherently

Sine qua non: Without which not. An essential condition, something that is indispensable; without which it could not be.

Stare decisis: Stand by things decided. The doctrine that, when a court has once laid down a principle of law applicable to a certain set of facts, it will adhere to that principle and apply it to future cases where the facts are substantially the same. This is a defining characteristic of the common law system.

compiled with the help of *Nolo's Legal Dictionary* at http:www.nolo.com/lawcenter/ dictionary/wordindex.cfm

Index of Cases

Index

Grievous harm 1, 143-145
Guilt, admission of 7, 17, 18, 25
Guilty, plea of 17, 18, 19, 40, 41, 145

H
Harm, definition of 135
    intention to 145
Hastening the death of a dying person 34
HIV/AIDS, Criminal law and 147-150
Homicide, definition of 1
    contributing causes to 28
    common intention in 59
    ingredients common to 5-38
    lawful, examples of 1
    relating to infants and unborn children
    124-128
unlawful, examples of 4
human being, definition of 5

I
Infanticide 1, 124-125
    burden of proof in 124
Intention *see* also Specific intent
    and Grievous bodily harm 129
Intoxication 48-50

K
Killing an unborn child 128
    to prevent serious crime 3
    accidental 3

L
Lawful corrections 137-139
Life, definition of beginning of 5

M
Malice aforethought 41-59
    and circumstantial evidence 53
    and mob justice 63
    and the body of the injured person 53,
    56-7
    and the conduct of the accused 52
    and the use of weapons 55-7, 60
    in attempted murder 68
    definition of 41
    failure to prove 59
    proof of 51-3, 57-9
    transferred 42

Manslaughter 1, 59, 89-92, 129-50
    Involuntary 129-131
    Voluntary 89-92
Medical evidence 6, 7, 10, 11, 14, 17, 19,-21,
    24, 27-30, 32, 37, 57, 67, 76, 77, 82, 127,
    143, 144, 145
Mens rea 39, 42, 133, 135, 148
Murder, offence of 1, 39-65
    and intoxication 48-50
    attempt to 66-7

N
Neglect, effect of 30
Negligence, effect of 130
Non-fatal assaults 1, 132-150

P
Passion, heat of 97-100
Plea of guilty 17, 18, 19, 40, 41, 145
Post mortem 7, 10, 19, 20, 23, 24, 26, 27, 31,
    44, 57, 62, 117
Proof of death 7, 27, 160
    by medical evidence 27, 28
    by confession of the accused 11
    by evidence of eyewitnesses 10
    through circumstantial evidence 7
    through production of a death certificate
    7
Property, defences based on protection of
    122
  self-defence and 118
Provocation 90-102
    adultery as 103
    and accused's age 96
    and definition of an ordinary and/or
    reasonable person 95
    and cultural background 95
    and property 104
    and self-defence 93
    and sex of the offender 96
    and voluntary mansalaughter 89-114
    defence of 89, 93
    legal effect of 9057
    relevance of physical characteristics to
    96
    retaliation for 101
    tests for 94, 95
    verbal insults as 103
    witchcraft as 105-110

www.ingramcontent.com/pod-product-compliance
Lightning Source LLC
Chambersburg PA
CBHW080250030426
42334CB00023BA/2761